how to butter toast

Pavilion
An imprint of HarperCollinsPublishers
Ltd
1 London Bridge Street
London SE1 9GF

www.harpercollins.co.uk

HarperCollinsPublishers
1st Floor, Watermarque Building
Ringsend Road Dublin 4
Ireland

10 9 8 7 6 5 4 3 2

First published in Great Britain by
Pavilion, an imprint of
HarperCollinsPublishers Ltd 2023

ISBN 978-0-00-855471-2

MIX
Paper | Supporting
responsible forestry
FSC
www.fsc.org   FSC™ C007454

This book is produced from
independently certified FSC™ paper
to ensure responsible forest
management.

For more information visit:
www.harpercollins.co.uk/green

Printed and bound in Latvia
by PNB Print

Publishing Director: Stephanie Milner
Commissioning Editor: Lucy Smith
Assistant Editor: Ellen Simmons
Senior Designer: Alice Kennedy-Owen
Illustrator: Alec Doherty
Artworker: Hannah Naughton
Copy editor: Angela Koo
Proofreader: Kate Reeves-Brown
Production controller: Grace O'Byrne

When using kitchen appliances
please always follow the
manufacturer's instructions

Tara Wigley

foreword by
Yotam Ottolenghi

how to butter toast

rhymes in a book
that help you to cook

PAVILION

Recipes, recipes, recipes. So many recipes! Too many recipes? As one who makes a respectable living from them I shouldn't be uttering such heresy, right? But I am also aware that we are inundated with them, that they are *everywhere*. It's the quantity and the prescriptiveness that can make you feel constrained, obliged to follow contradictory directions, lost and a bit confused.

In comes Tara and tells you not to worry... and to be happy. Not to worry, because even the greatest minds rarely agree on anything, there *are* so many ways to make porridge, all 100 per cent legit, so you don't need to fret about getting it just so. Read some advice, listen to experts, get a little insight, and then find your own way! Different strokes, etc.

Be happy, because there is so much fun to be had from reading Tara's sharp verses, getting in on the internal debates and inner wrangling between professionals about what a great gravy really consists of, or, actually, what different gravies consist of.

There really is something liberating in learning a thing or two, often way more, about food from reading a piece of light poetry. It's all about making cooking accessible. You *can* become a better cook, a more knowledgeable and confident one, whilst chuckling away to yourself and enjoying one of the many perceptions and scientific snippets here.

This book is full of practical advice. I bet you'll find an endless list of facts you never knew, or never knew you needed to know. You'll find insights that will inform your cooking, or just inform *you,* like that room temperature eggs will get your mayonnaise to emulsify more easily, or that vinegar won't (so add it at the end).

Simple dishes are often the most contentious. Everyone has an opinion. But, paradoxically, it's not the 'either/or' where the answer often lies, but in the 'this *or* that', and it is you that gets to choose between them. It's the canned *or* fresh tomatoes, the butter *or* the oil, the basil *or* oregano (in the case of tomato sauce) that will liberate your mind, and it is all expertly seasoned with Tara's wit and charm.

Yotam Ottolenghi

introduction:
a recipe book without recipes

This is a book about recipes, with very few recipes in it.
'A recipe book without recipes?! What, therefore, is in it?'

It looks at some of the different ways the same dish is prepared
to reassure the general cook that they should not feel scared.

For all that chefs make out that their way is the 'gospel' text,
different versions of the 'gospel' leave one quite perplexed.

It is, in fact, the *recipes* that can mess with the mind;
with all their little differences, they end up misaligned.

The fewer the ingredients, the fewer items used,
the more chefs seem so certain, and the more we are confused.

'Definitive' turns out to be not quite so watertight,
there are in fact a lot of ways to make a dish 'just right'.

If you think the way you make it tastes divine to you,
then this is how it 'should' be cooked; this is what you
    'should' do.

There is a lot of noise out there, there are a lot of cooks
saying lots of things online and lots of things in books.

So here's to seeing recipes, as preference not default:
instructions read with quite a hearty pinch of (flaked sea) salt…

Melted butter on hot toast and served up on a plate.
It seems like nothing, really, could be clearer or more straight.
But though, in terms of things required, the number is just two,
there is a lot of wiggle room for what there is to do.

The first thing that must happen is to make the call and choose
from all the breads available, which one to buy and use.
Those who want some texture that is light and open go,
quite often, for a tangy white and crusty sourdough.

The slices must be cut quite thick, for if they are too little,
they'll turn, when cooked, to husks, which will then crack and
    be all brittle.
Once a decent slice is cut, it's time to add some heat
(without which there would be no toast to butter, *nor* to eat).

There are some toaster-sceptics who do *not* think they're
    so great.
'Too often what they do to bread is just incinerate.
A better choice is oven-grill, in which things can't go wrong!'
Others, though, are not convinced and think it takes too long.

'Heating up the oven-grill is always such a faff!
There is no morning time to spare – we need to leave the gaff!
The toaster's simply quicker, it can, frankly, not be beaten:
you put the bread in, turn it on and – boom! – it can be eaten.'

When it comes to toast-related gadgets and invention
the toaster's *not* the biggest bone of etiquette convention.
The toast rack takes place number one, where toast stands
    side-by-side:
this is, it seems, the ultimate strong-feeling great-divide.

'The toast goes hard and cold,' the no-crowd shake their
    heads and mutter,
'which means it's not set up, at all, to take in melting butter'.
'That's the beauty of cold toast, which has to wait its turn,'
says the toast-rack fan, who likes their toast all cold and firm.

'Being cold and crunchy means that there's a natural stop.
The butter won't dissolve and melt and sits, instead, on top.
There's very little better than some butter that sits tight,
topped with jam or marmalade – this is toast done just right'.

Thinking through the butter, though, it's clear most are agreed
that butter is the only fat that toast will ever need.
Very few who know what's what will ever choose the route,
where margarine or veggie spread is used as substitute.

Be the butter Lurpak or an Irish Kerrygold,
just make sure that it's pretty soft; it won't spread if too cold.
The knife to spread with should, ideally, have an edge
    that's smooth,
though butter knives feel, maybe, like there's something
    still to prove?

Those who make a case for their beloved butter knives,
will claim that, when it comes to toast, they lead such stress-
    free lives.
'We never need to get all cross or in a toasted flutter,
resulting from those pesky crumbs that get stuck in the butter.'

'Once the butter, with our knife, goes first onto a plate,
it means that it is very easy to avoid this fate.
Another knife can then be used and take it on from here,
so the pat of butter stays crumb-free: clean and fresh and clear.'

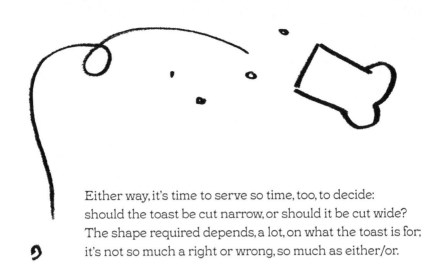

Either way, it's time to serve so time, too, to decide:
should the toast be cut narrow, or should it be cut wide?
The shape required depends, a lot, on what the toast is for;
it's not so much a right or wrong, so much as either/or.

If it's due a spread of jam, then there will be a case
for triangles, as these will help keep jam off from the face.
The pointy edges of the shape will help the eater eat,
so triangles, with sticky things, will keep things nice and neat.

If the toast is being made to take a form of topping,
(with some eggs, for instance, which require a bit of mopping).
In this instance, triangles are altogether wrong,
the need is for a rectangle, something hardy and quite strong.

Soldiers, though, for boiled eggs are clearly just a 'must',
whichever shape is made, be sure to keep hold of the crust.
It brings a welcome contrast and it brings a happy crunch
to what is often at the base of breakfast, supper or some lunch.

how to

make

a cup of tea

Who would have thought that it could be a simple cup of tea,
that would incite such strength of feeling and controversy?
That this simplest of all questions, asking, 'how do you
     take yours?'
can let loose such a big, hot stream of 'do' and 'don't' tea bores.

And that's the case, regardless of the tea with which
     we're dealing.
It's just the same with PG Tips or finest leaf Darjeeling.
Where there exists a tea leaf that is due a hot infusion,
there's always quite a lot of room for tea-drinking confusion.

Are bags okay? In their defence, they bring a burst of colour.
Though versus loose-leaf, flavour-wise, they will be
     slightly duller.
And once the bag is in there, then how long to leave and brew?
To 'steep' is fine, but it is not okay to sit and let it 'stew'.

Three, four, five minutes is fine, inside a pre-warmed pot,
with water that has been poured on (*just less* than
   boiling hot).
When it comes to water, this may well in fact just be,
the *most* important factor when it comes to quality.

For if the water from the tap is 'hard' this will become
(when on the surface of the tea) just good old-fashioned scum.
Investing in a water filter can be funds well spent,
if scum-on-tea is something that you are keen to prevent.

The biggest source of conflict, though, for those who have
   a thirst,
is whether it's the milk or water that should go in first.
Those who put the milk in first put weight upon the fact
that water first, if boiling hot, might make the china crack.
Though china is less commonplace, these days, and mugs
   are strong,
the 'milk first' lot still find the 'milk last' crowd just simply wrong.

The 'milk last' crew will counter with the fact that they all think
that it allows much more control of strength within the drink.
Milk in first leaves much to chance; milk last removes the stress.
Those who like it weak add lots (and fans of strong add less).

The milk geeks, on this single point, have only just begun.
For them that simple summary is just class 101.
The matter is not simply one to state a preference,
some basic science can be used to mount a clear defence.

For milk is full of proteins and these will then, therefore, be
denatured when they're boiled and, do so, most unevenly.
This makes milk clump together and it makes it taste all 'boiled',
and a surface skin can form, which makes the cup of tea
    look spoiled.
Cold milk, instead, when added first will slow the speed
    of change,
the taste will be more even and the look will be less strange.

A big mug in the morning, then a china cup for tea?
Is this the way fine etiquette would deem things best to be?
Sugar, yes? Or sugar, no? Would you like one or two?
The choices that you make for tea say much, it seems, of you.

Whether you're a 'builder's' or a 'fine-leaf artisan',
this cup of infused water can be really partisan.
It also is a balm, remember: one to cure life's ails,
the thing that we all think to make when everything else fails.
So maybe don't brew over, *too much*, what is 'right' or 'wrong':
just fill the kettle up with water; put that kettle on.

how to make

porridge

Before we even start to stir, the thing to know should be
that oats come in a range – there's not just one variety.

They can be whole or rolled or quick; they can be called
    pinhead –
it's all a lot to take in when *you've* just rolled out of bed.
They can be instant, steel-cut, oatmeal or the large jumbo,
but break it down, it's all okay: here's what you need to know.

Rolled oats are those that are steamed and flattened after that.
Quick oats are just steamed for longer and then made more flat.
The process is the same – the rolled oats take a little longer
when cooking as they're processed less, so are a little stronger.

Jumbo oats are big rolled oats (the clue is in the name).
Pinhead oats and steel-cut oats are actually the same!
You'll see both names when seeking oats and standing in
    the shop,
but they are both just hulled oat groats, which have then
    got the chop.

They don't get steamed or flattened; they are wholly
 unprocessed,
so for the porridge puritans they'll always be the best.
For many, though, they'll always have a little too much bite;
a mix of steel-cut and oatmeal will, therefore, be just right.

There are three ways in which oatmeal is made and can
 be found:
coarse or fine or medium: it's just oats that are ground.
The more that they are ground, the smoother they will also be.
Some will like this, some will not, and find it too gloopy.

The more you stir oats as they cook (folklore dictates
 clockwise),
the more the starch within the oats will then gelatinize.
When it comes to stirring, a thin 'spurtle' does the trick –
a spurtle, really, being just a baton or a stick.

The theory is that standard wooden spoons are prone to crush
and turn the cooking porridge oats into a baby mush.
Though those without a spurtle need not don a sad-face frown,
just take a wooden spoon and simply turn it upside down.

21

The length of time that people say your oats will need to cook
varies wildly with each person, pan and oat and book.
Some will swear the oats need soaking for a whole long night;
others say an hour or two (or none) will be alright.
Cooking times can range from just five minutes to an hour
(that's a lot to fit in if you want a morning shower).

The liquid they get cooked in is the source of much debate,
with water-only deemed okay for puritans to sate.
A mix of water and some milk has many fans who pitch
the case that milk, just by itself, is always far too rich.
Milk to water, one-to-two – that is the ratio
that a lot of porridge people think the way to go.

The ratio of oats to liquid is not something fixed,
it varies if the oats are ground or whole or cut or mixed.
Pinheads need a lot more liquid than, say, fine oatmeal:
you'll need to have a play around to get the proper feel.

When it comes to toppings, all opinions are strong.
For some, the move beyond plain salt is thought to be
   just wrong.
Others like a sugar crunch and sprinkle with good cheer,
baffled as to why some versions are quite so austere.

Demerara, golden syrup, honey, fruit compote
are some of the options for the sweet-tooth porridge lot.
Grated apple, chopped-up dates, perhaps some
    tempting cream,
this is hale and hearty porridge, promising the dream.

There are, also, a lot of ways to take things savoury:
soft-boiled egg and soya sauce meet in a rice congee.
Melted butter, chopped-up chives, some grated cheddar cheese
is another way to go if savoury will please.

So when it comes to porridge, just do what floats your boat –
this is an easygoing grain, the humble little oat.
There's room for all the Quakers and for all the John McCanns
(heck, even Ready Brek has got its dedicated fans).

how to tell how old your egg is

Finding out if your egg's fresh (or if it's past the brink)
can be established in some water: does it float or sink?

For eggshells are so porous (thanks to being super thin)
that they can both let water out and also take air in.

The older that they are, therefore, the more air's in to bloat,
so when it's put in water it will always, ergo, float.

A fresh egg, on the other hand, has little air inside,
so it will sink, and stay down low, and lie out on its side.

how to

boil an

egg

This is the most subjective egg, in that the white and yolk
can be 'just right' for one person and for the next, 'a joke'.
For it can be 'just firm' or 'firm' or 'liquid' or 'well-set',
it varies if the egg's 'well-done' or if it's to be 'wet'.

If 'right' is not a fixed thing then it's safer to agree
on what we *don't* want from our eggs, how they should never be.

We *never* want our shells to crack, when cooking in the pot;
we *never* want our whites to feel in any way like snot.
We never want them rubbery (that means they're overdone).
These things are all considered right by (nearly) everyone.

Everyone agrees, as well, that eggs should not be old,
and shells can crack if eggs are cooked straight from the
    fridge (too cold).
Another reason for cracked shells is if the cook forgot
that boiling water will, always, be really *very* hot!

If the egg goes in the water when it's at a boil,
just do it gently – use a spoon – and then the shell won't spoil.
Some go further and suggest an extra step to take:
to prick a pin in at the top to let the steam escape.

Others think it's madness to go in at the boiling stage,
that egg and water need to start off at the same (cool) page.
Proponents of this method (of the egg in at the start)
have got their timings down to what they see as quite an art.

But even in this camp, it seems, that no one is agreed:
should the water heat up slow or really go for speed?
The king of science, Heston B, says 'Go! Fast as you can!
The egg just covered, heat on max and lid stays on the pan!

As soon as bubbles first appear, remove it from the heat,
leave it for six minutes and then you are set to eat.'
Heston B points out to us that, paradoxically,
boiled eggs, if they are truly boiled, will end up rubbery.

For whites will set much sooner than their yellow, yolky friend,
which means that rubber will always be whitey's boiled end.
So, it turns out, the way to boil an egg is *not* to boil it;
doing so will be the thing that will, in fact, just spoil it.

So, egg in the pan, water on top, bring it to a simmer,
set aside and wait a while (go make some toast for dinner).

Timings here are something that each person has to learn,
depending on the preferences for 'runny' versus 'firm'.

Four minutes tends to be the guide, but practise lots at home;
make boiled eggs the dish that you perfect when on your own.
For boiling eggs is something that will simply just divide
(might be best to scrap plan A and think of doing fried).

how to

poach

an egg

An egg cooked just in water (which is also known as poached)
is something that, for many, is an egg dish never broached.
Fried or boiled or scrambled: yes! – these are all fine and great,
yet poachers seem to be the eggs that can intimidate.

It should be simple: heat the water, crack the egg straight in,
but should the water be left still or set to a fast spin?
The spinning fans will tell you it's the spin that helps to make
the egg keep hold of its neat oval, teardrop 'eggy' shape.

'For going in the whirlpool', say the vortex-loving folk,
'means that the egg white wraps around the inner yellow yolk.
The water must be simmering, the whirl it must be brisk,
don't use a wooden spoon to stir, it's best to use a whisk.'

Some leave the egg to simmer there for quite a little while,
while others think this makes no sense – it does not reconcile
the fact that agitation means the egg can fall apart,
so why not cook them in still water from the very start?

Bring the water to the boil and then turn off the heat.
Add the eggs and let them chill, they'll get cooked
   and stay neat.
Proponents of this 'heat and leave' way (crack it in and wait)
think that the water whirling round will only complicate.
Use a spoon to turn the eggs, the method never fails,
and means you don't end up with eggs with straggly white tails.

Others say they know the secret to avoid such pain,
and that's to put the whole egg in a fine mesh sieve to strain.
All the loose white you don't want will just fall down
   straight through,
the yolk stays put, the white is tight: the two are stuck like glue.
The sieve can then be lowered straight into the water pot,
the cooking process starts thanks to the water, which is hot.

All of this lot are united in *not* being fans
of the use of any kind of metal poaching pans.
'The thing about a poaching pan', says anti-poach-pan team,
'is that the eggs aren't really poached – they're cooked more
   by the steam.
And by the time the inside yolk is set and cooked enough,
the outside white is far too firm, it's rubbery and tough.'

'To wash the pan, too, is a drag!', the anti-pan types mutter.
'Alleviated', pro-pans say, 'by just a knob of butter.
Simply added just before the egg is cracked straight in,
   the lack of hassle's *more* than worth it for a firm-ish skin.'

Never shall the twain meet here, there'll always be a feud
regarding whether 'poached' eggs have to be cooked 'in
   the nude'.

Freshness is the crucial thing, for it determines whether
the whites, when cracked into the water, will be held together.
The older that the egg you have, the 'looser' is its white,
and what you want's the *opposite*: you want it to be tight.

The older that an egg becomes, the more it's alkaline;
adding in some acid will, then, help things stay in line.
Just a drop of vinegar – a cup would be a waste
(and means your egg would have a very vinegary taste).

The need for fresh eggs is the one thing totally agreed,
beyond that there are several ways to do the poaching deed.
So whether you're a vortex fan or don't want any friction,
practice is what's needed here (and cracking with conviction).

Some first crack eggs into a cup, this always works quite well:
the eggs are slipped into the water, with no risk of shell.
Others line a ramekin with clingfilm lightly oiled –
it's good for cooking eggs in bulk but, looks-wise, rather spoiled.
The eggs in clingfilm look a bit like old-school fun-fair fish
(not perhaps the look to go for with your breakfast dish).

If you want to cook ahead, it's possible to do –
run them under cold water, then, to serve, just warm through.
It means you can poach, judgement-free, and feel like a top host
when serving up eggs Benedict or ramen (or fresh toast).

how to

scramble

eggs

scrambled styles

A timer is not needed, nor a fancy poaching pan,
for scrambled eggs need little skill as these are eggs that can
just be mixed up (that's 'scrambled') and then perched upon
    some heat:
mixed and stirred (that's 'scrambled more') then plate up, sit
    down, eat!

But these are *eggs* so thoughts abound, of course, on how
    they're done,
with different dos and don'ts (and won'ts) put forth by everyone.
For eggs are so protean that there's not one way to be;
how 'things are done' depends on plans for their consistency.

There are three types of scrambled eggs: all come from
    different schools,
all with their own distinct and very different set of rules.
The fundamental thing, which changes how they feel and look,
is *when* the eggs are stirred or if they're left to set and cook.

First up, we have the soft, loose type: the 'fancy French affair' –
stirred so much, it's purée-like; the curds are barely there.
The beaten eggs are put into a saucepan that is cold,
the heat is then kept very low and then we whisk: don't fold!

For folding would entrap *more* air, which here needs to escape.
It's getting out the air, through whisking, that will help to make
the egg proteins stay close and tight, it's custard-like in look.
The wires on the whisk cut through the eggs as they slow-cook.

Those who want their scrambled eggs to not be quite
    so smooth
are less intense about the need to keep things on the move.
For stirring them less frequently will help the eggs to get
some curds (and texture), which appear when they are left
    to set.

So these are eggs – the second type – summed up by
    certain words:
'softly scrambled', 'not too dense', with 'delicate, small curds'.
They start off, like the first type, in a pan that is unheated
(if it's hot, the eggs will seize and set, thus be defeated).

It helps, as well, to choose a pan with a surface that's quite wide,
it makes the curds form quickly if there is some space inside.
The heat is more like 'medium' than 'barely-there-so-low'
but, still, these eggs are not rushed through, they are cooked
    long and slow.

Like the heat (on medium) the stirring's 'in between' –
it's regular (not constant), which, for texture, will then mean
it's neither 'custard-fancy-French', nor curds all large and dry
(such curds result from when the heat is, from the
    start, set high).

Leaving them alone a while is for this third type key,
so once the eggs are in the pan then they are left to be.
For left alone they will trap air that will expand with heat
(which would, of course, deflate with every whisk and stir
    and beat).

Folding gently is the way to help the eggs expand;
puffing up requires a real lightness of the hand.
So that's the general principle, the basic rule of thumb:
leave the eggs alone a while and fluffy they'll become.

the rules

Beyond these general stirring rules there are some other
    choices,
each of which have champions, who all have their own voices.
There are, however, basic things, upon which most agree –
that eggs, for instance, should, per person, range from two
    to three.
Unless you love your washing up, the pan should be non-stick,
and microwaves are not okay, however clean and quick.

Ten grams of butter for two eggs and there will be few moans.
Add it to the pan and leave until the butter foams.
The eggs, before they hit the pan, should *gently* be combined;
if over-whisked and runny they will, as the chef will find,
end up tougher when they cook, a toughness that just means
coagulation's gone too far for all those egg proteins.
For cooking scrambled eggs is all about protein control,
aided or impeded by what else is in the bowl.

Pre-salting, for example, is, for most, a thumbs-up-YES!
It stops the proteins linking tight, which leads to tenderness.
A little splash of water is, for fluffy eggs, a dream:
more vapour means big bubbles, which means lighter, which
    will mean
the eggs will puff up nicely (though you'll hear the milk defender,
saying that some dairy's needed to help make them tender).
For milk or cream both have the fat to stop those forming bonds,
so are – for fluffy, tender eggs – the magic, scrambled wands.

Some find the cream a little rich, a bit too much to eat,
preferring to, instead, stir through crème fraîche when
    off the heat.
It only needs a teaspoon to enrich and make it smooth;
it also cools the eggs down so, in doing, it will prove
to be a useful way of making sure that everyone
receives their eggs before they're dry and, frankly, overdone.
A little knob of butter works, like cream, and does the trick,
making sure the cooking stops and does so nice and quick.

Take the pan off from the heat, before you're set to serve.
The eggs cook on, just in the pan, so hold on to your nerve.
Remember, also, that the pan can always be returned,
but 'overcooked' can't be undone, as we have all, once, learned.

Finish off with chopped fresh herbs or freshly grated cheese,
chilli flakes or paprika – just add here what you please.
If serving them with veggie sides, that's fine and good and great,
just make sure that the veg don't leak onto the eggy plate.

If you're serving up for friends, make sure that you're the host
who finds out if it's 'on' or 'next to' when it comes to toast.
For some *this* is the big debate, the source of pain and pride:
if eggs are served on top of toast or sitting on the side...

how to fry an egg

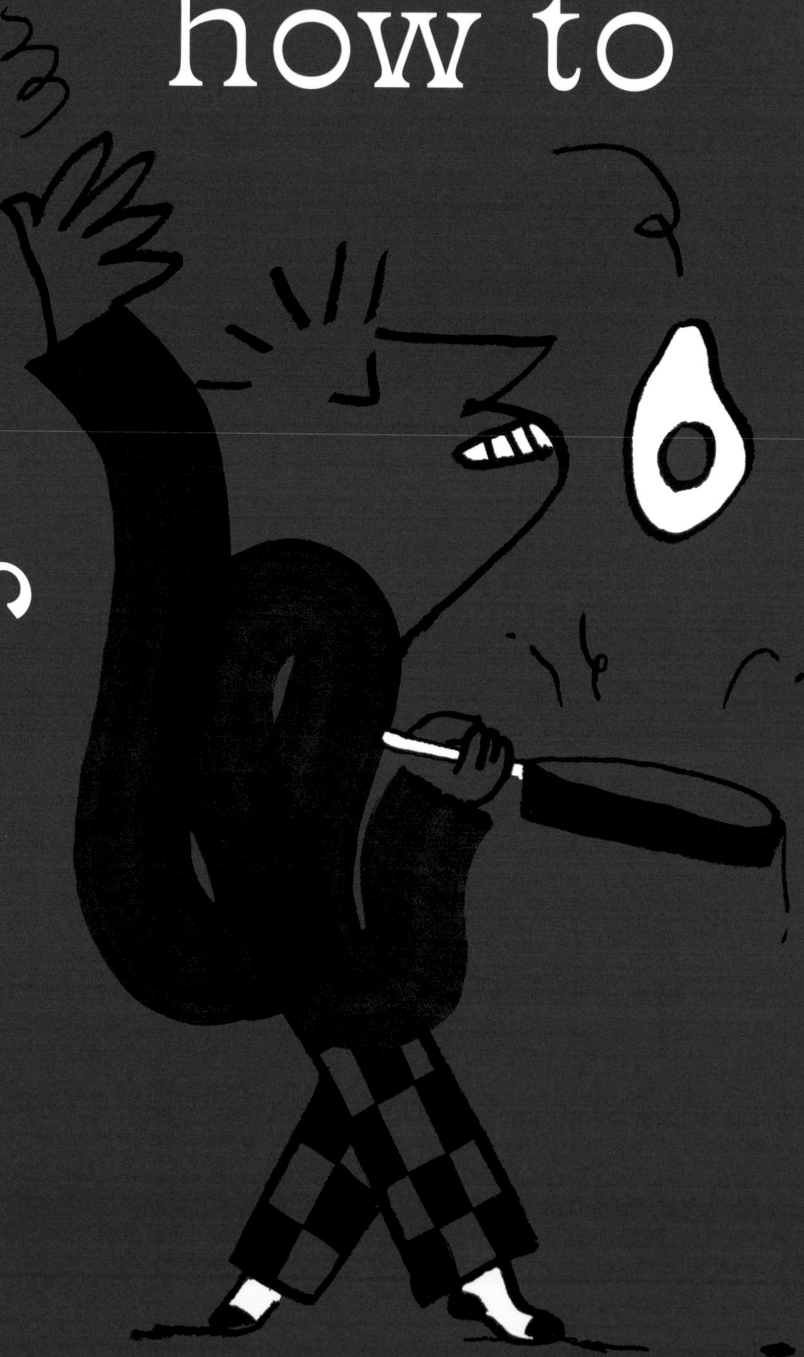

There are, for those who like fried eggs, two general
   fried-egg schools –
each have their own supporters and their own firm set of rules.

The first school wants some *texture* and in order to be 'fried',
the whites should have some bubbles and be crisp on
   the outside.
They may not look so pretty (with the whites more brown
   than white),
but when it comes to frying eggs then this is 'things done right'.

'Au contraire', says team soft-white, 'this is an egg disgrace!
Eating that is tantamount to chewing brittle lace.
The white's too thin, the sides are burnt, the whole
   thing's decimated;
this Spanish-*huevos-fritos*-style is hugely overrated!'

Those who want their white to be all silken, smooth and clean
are aiming for a look that is more formal and pristine.
The white is creamy sustenance, the edges don't look hurt,
the yolk is sitting happily: it's orange, intact, pert.

Within both schools there are some rules to follow by the book,
for example, 'fresh' is best for how the egg will cook.
For when the egg is really fresh, its proteins will be stronger,
which means that it will hold together for a little longer.
This then stops it spreading thinly after it's been cracked:
in the pan it will stay neat – substantial and compact.

(Another way to curb the spread is always to begin
by cracking the egg into a cup and, from there, sliding in.
The entry's much more gentle: it's a little more precise.
For those who want a thicker white, this can be really nice.)

As well as starting off with eggs that are not very old,
you also want to start with eggs that are not really cold.
If they're cold the white will take a longer time to set,
after which a 'too-firm' yolk is what you're prone to get.

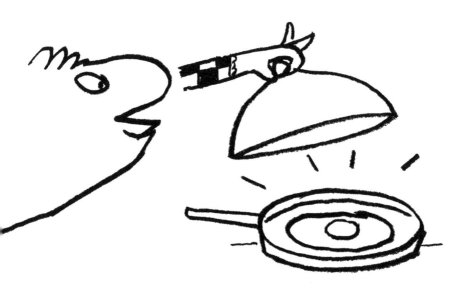

If they come straight from the fridge, the egg exacerbates
the problem of all whites and yolks, which set at different rates.
The yolks start setting sooner, so cook on as they wait
for the whites to set (around degree mark sixty-eight).

The heat is also only coming from one way (the base) –
so that's another challenge that all fried eggs have to face.
Helping the top side to set without the heat to haste
can be achieved by covering or flipping or a baste.

Those who use a cover like the fact that this will mean
the egg, as well as frying, will then also get a steam.
Some might add a cube of ice: 'It melts', we will be told.
This way of making steam is known as cooking eggs 'blindfold'.

It works as well without the ice, if you are not a fan –
just use a lid that is more narrow than the frying pan.
That way it's on the pan base, so the space to fill is small;
the steam can quickly form and rise and, after that, then fall.

Flipping is another way to give the top some heat,
but some will always see this method as a fried-egg 'cheat'.
'Easy-over' means the top is certainly well set,
but often it gets sealed so much, the yolk's no longer wet.
This works well for a sandwich, where leakage is a mess,
but generally we want our yolks to be cooked *somewhat* less.

This is where the basting method can, then, work a treat.
It cooks the whites but also leaves the yolks all nice and neat.
Once the egg is sizzling, the pan gets tilted up,
the fat then pools and can be scooped up with a spoon or cup.
It's drizzled neatly over and the white cooks evenly –
for many it's the only way that fried eggs ought to be.

In addition to these three ways, there is one we've missed:
'how to fry an egg if you're a chef-come-modernist'.
Separating yolk from white is what they do to get
the white cooked perfectly and with a yolk that is just set.
The white goes first into the pan and cooks uninterrupted
before the yolk is added back: the egg is reconstructed!

Heston B does this (of course), learnt from Bernard Loiseau,
the French chef for whom perfect was the only way to go.
For many, though, such deconstruction is far from ideal
for what is meant to be a quick and easy fast-food meal.

We've come this far without a mention ('Shocking', some
    will mutter)
of the pros and cons of using oil compared to butter.
Either works for frying eggs, so both are fine to use
but if you're wanting richness, then it's butter you
    should choose.
Olive oil is fruity, which is great when eggs will be
served on top of lunch or supper when it's savoury.

The *way* you cook your egg will also help you to decide.
Oil is what you need if what you want is *really* fried.
The frying pan can heat awhile, the oil gets really hot,
so when the egg goes in, the time it needs is not a lot.

Unless you want it 'Spanish-style', your eggs don't need
    to drown,
too much oil and what was white will soon be turned to brown.
Starting with a non-stick pan reduces how much oil
you need to help ensure your egg won't stick (and
    therefore spoil).

If it's butter being used, a little knob is fine,
though frying eggs with butter will then need some extra time.
If the heat is medium and if a lid is on,
around about three minutes and your egg won't go far wrong.

Season as it leaves the pan and serve it straight away –
enjoy the fried-egg moment and then crack on with your day!

how to

make

pancakes

Recipes for batter vary slightly, book to book,
depending on the palate of each different pancake cook.
A simple rule of thumb, for all, will surely always be
the one where all you need to do is count out 'one, two, three'.

ONE hundred grams of flour and then TWO large eggs
    cracked in,
THREE hundred mills of full-fat milk (you don't want
    semi-skim).
A tablespoon of sunflower oil, a little pinch of salt,
whisk until it's nice and smooth and then your whisk
    should halt.

(There's no need to keep whisking on, combined is
    quite enough;
stirring more makes gluten form, which makes the
    pancakes tough).
If you want your pancakes fluffy, at their perfect best,
leave them here – about an hour – just for the mix to rest.

The reason for the rest is that it gives the proteins time,
the liquid gets absorbed and then the bubbles can align.
These bubbles can next rise up and then make their
    great escape;
a batter without bubbles will help make a smooth pancake.

The resting of the mixture gives you time, which you can take
to focus on the toppings and the fillings you will make.
Choose if you are going for a savoury or sweet;
use up what you have, or what is up your favourite street.

Nice and simple – it's a classic — sugar with some lemon.
Or chocolate will, for many, be the perfect-pancake heaven.
Wilted greens are lovely, mixed up with some grated cheese,
but this is pancake DIY, so do just as you please.

When it comes to cooking them, the pan should be quite hot,
greased with butter (or some oil), there need not be a lot.
Ladle in some batter, just a cover on the base.
Let it cook: it needs to stay awhile, fixed in one place.

Once the edges start to brown, you're ready then to flip.
Have conviction – go for it! – you must be nice and quick!
Once it's flipped, return the heat, just half a minute's fine.
Serve it up or keep it warm and flip another time.

Repeat with all the batter and you grease more as you go –
your pancakes will get better as you get into the flow.
Don't worry if the first few are not perfect and all neat:
these can be seen as practice (also known as 'the cook's treat')…

how to peel banana

(and other things)

Peeling a banana, if it's ripe and speckled brown
is done best if the fruit is turned completely upside down.
The stem is held in one hand, so the second hand is spare
to squeeze the nubby tip so that it opens with no tear.

Monkeys have been doing this, all the way along.
Our two-year-olds were right, in fact, when screaming we
     were wrong,
for being heedless parents and just ruining their day
by peeling their banana in *completely* the wrong way!

It's not just little people, who go through this tantrum hell,
we all get close when peeling eggs that have that 'sticky' shell.
The way to help prevent this, is to check when they are sold:
they tend to peel more easily when they're a few days old.

Another thing that you can do to help the shells play nice
is crack your cooked egg in a bowl of water with some ice.
The shock of the cold water will then shrink the white enough
that water seeps beneath the film and it's no longer tough.

Peppers also sit within the cook-then-cool peel team.
After roasting, they go in a covered bowl to steam.
Once they're cool enough to handle, all the pepper needs
is hands to pick away the skin and, with it, all the seeds.

This works as well for heads of garlic, large tomatoes too;
toss them in a little oil before they get cooked through.
Blanching is another way to get tomatoes peeled,
score the base with sharpened knife and see the flesh revealed.

For as the skin hits boiling water, it recoils right back –
they pretty much then peel themselves, a little kitchen hack.
Almonds also work with blanching, with no need to score
(a job, of course, that would be both a hassle and a bore).

Just blanch them for a minute, rinse, then use your fingertips
to give the loosened, shrivelled skin a sharpish little nip.
After this a little squeeze will ease the almond through.
It's a satisfying job to take the time to do.

Always fun to extricate are pomegranate seeds.
Slice the fruit from left to right, all that it next, then, needs
is to be held firm in one palm, with cut-side facing down –
bash it from the top and watch the jewels fall from the crown.
Do this with a bowl below to catch them as they fall
(and do this in a sink to save a mess splashed on the wall).

Knobs of ginger can be tricky with their stubby pieces –
use a teaspoon, which can get in all the folds and creases.
Scraping with the teaspoon's edge is better than a knife,
the whole root can get used and prepped with very little strife.

A knife is very useful, though, as avocados prove
when it comes to their big stones, and how best to remove.
Once you've cut your fruit in half you whack the stone head-on
with the sharp edge of a knife, you twist and pull – it's gone!

What you must not ever do is stab it with the tip:
this will often miss the stone and from there it will slip.
Such a move might cause the piercing of a palm or wrist.
Remember then, it's 'whack not stab' – followed by a twist.

Onions do not benefit from either 'stab' or 'whack' –
training (or just practice) will reveal the simple knack.
Slice the bulb straight down the middle, starting at the stem,
end up at the root with two halves that are ready then
to have their paper outer layers simply peeled away
before each half is laid down flat (it's firm now and will stay).

It's ready for the final stage, the slicing or the chopping:
the stage that shows the choices that were made when out
    knife-shopping.
For it is worth investing here, though they come at a price,
you really want a knife to do its job and cleanly slice.

For fingers when they're cut or sliced can take an age to heal,
so take the time to really learn to chop and slice and peel...

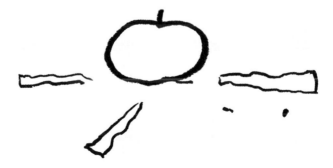

how to

dress

a salad

It's basically a bowl of leaves tossed in a simple dressing.
So why does salad seem to keep so many people guessing?
Leaves get drenched or dressed too soon – before they're
   even tried,
the salad's relegated, it just sits there on the side.

There is a world in which (as leafy salad lovers know)
salad leaves *can* be the dish to really steal the show.
So if we want to help our salad be the lunchtime star,
let's break it down and look at what the rules and top tips are.

The first tip might seem obvious but, still, it's good to state
that starting off with *tasty* leaves will help things to taste great.
Where you shop or what you grow, from here all
   things commence,
the impact of this first step is definitive – immense!

Once you have your chosen leaf, you also need to choose
the dressing that goes with it, it would be no good to use
something really creamy on a leaf too weak to hold.
Such dressing needs a robust leaf like kale: big and bold.

There are three types of dressing that most leaves will tend
   to get:
the creamy type, the dairy-based, the simple vinaigrette.

The vinaigrette – a French dressing – is one that is well built
for leaves that are quite precious and are prone to quickly wilt.
Rocket, for example, is a leaf that cannot stand
dressings that are creamy, or made with a heavy hand.

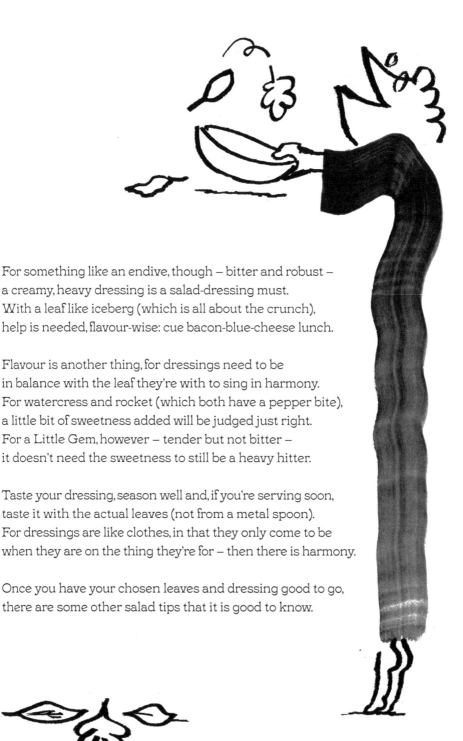

For something like an endive, though – bitter and robust –
a creamy, heavy dressing is a salad-dressing must.
With a leaf like iceberg (which is all about the crunch),
help is needed, flavour-wise: cue bacon-blue-cheese lunch.

Flavour is another thing, for dressings need to be
in balance with the leaf they're with to sing in harmony.
For watercress and rocket (which both have a pepper bite),
a little bit of sweetness added will be judged just right.
For a Little Gem, however – tender but not bitter –
it doesn't need the sweetness to still be a heavy hitter.

Taste your dressing, season well and, if you're serving soon,
taste it with the actual leaves (not from a metal spoon).
For dressings are like clothes, in that they only come to be
when they are on the thing they're for – then there is harmony.

Once you have your chosen leaves and dressing good to go,
there are some other salad tips that it is good to know.

Put your leaves into a bowl about three times their size:
it will look vast but you will see such scaling up is wise.
For salad should be tossed by hand, tongs never should
    be used.
They'll hurt the tender, precious leaves, which will be left
    all bruised.

Put some dressing in the bowl, add half or thereabout –
it's easier to add more later than to take it out.
(At the same time, holding back some leaves is never wrong –
to add them in if needed if the dressing *is* too strong.)

Use your hands to rub it in, to get an even coating.
Taste again and check for salt (a point always worth noting).
Serve as soon as you are done – however well it's built,
the 'salad days' don't last that long before they start to wilt.

how to

make a

vinaigrette

To make a basic vinaigrette, there's not a lot to do,
in terms of things you need to have, there are in fact just two.
Some vinegar's required (or lemon juice is fine to use),
plus oil (from which there is a range we get to pick and choose).

The classic choice for vinegar would tend to be red wine
(or white is often interchanged, which is completely fine).
Play around with different kinds: the tartness of a sherry
or Champagne's always fun to use (and makes things sound
    quite merry).

Balsamic has a sweetness that can work and really please
if your salad has some salty feta or some soft goat's cheese.
There's no need to restrain yourself to using only one,
choose a couple, mix and match – just taste and have some fun.

When it comes to choice of oil, things can get quite confused.
Should our extra-virgin be the one that's always used?
Some say 'Absolutely, it's the dressing heavy-hitter',
whilst others say that 'No! It will just make the dressing bitter'.

'Better', say the bitter lot, 'to use a neutral oil.
Extra-virgin is too much, it dominates, it spoils.
Use a light canola, or a groundnut is the thing,
they blend and also let the other dressing flavours sing.'

Some will take the middle ground and think that it is wise
to have a blend of different oils, a kind of compromise.
Two-to-one part (neutral-flavoured) is the ratio
that most consider as the way that oil mixes go.

Ratios remain a thing we need to keep in mind:
how much of what we want to mix, emulsify and bind.
Raymond Blanc sticks to the French rule that it's one-to-three
(one part acid, three parts oil – so not too vinegary),
with a little salt to start and pepper cracked to finish.
That is it! All else would merely distract and diminish.

Some prefer things more acidic, they like one-to-two.
On this point you have to taste and then choose what to do.
There are as many different oils as there are salad leaves,
so get stuck in and roll on up your dressing-making sleeves.

If we simply put these things together in a jar,
we'll find our dressing does not really get us very far.
For oil's less dense than vinegar, a fact that explains why
it floats above said vinegar: they won't emulsify.

Whisk the two together and, though briefly they'll combine,
they'll separate again – they split – in very little time.
These are two hostile parties, sharing only a revulsion,
mediation will be needed to create a strong emulsion.

As well as acting as a bond for disunited things,
emulsions also work well for the flavour that they bring.
Garlic, which is crushed, is great: it helps to stabilize,
but mustard is the one that wins the 'Best Emulsion' prize.

For a nice thick dressing it is hard to go far wrong
by following the French lead, and so, choosing their Dijon.
The yolk of egg's another route: the blend is thick and stays
(but some think that this pushes it towards a mayonnaise).
Other things here can be used: tahini works a dream,
tomato purée, miso, honey or a dash of cream.

Once our oil and acid have combined and are great mates,
enhancements can be added if we want to titivate.
Depending on your choices, you then work with what
    you've got:
if Dijon has been used then next consider chopped shallot.

Herbs and spices all work well, some mashed-up anchovies,
play around and you can really add here what you please.
Tweak and change your dressing so it fits your chosen feast,
make it Thai or Japanese or from the Middle East.

In terms of your proportions (if we're based on one-to-three),
then emulsion is a third (of one part) in its quantity.
Mix it with your vinegar and season at the start,
add a little sugar, if you don't like things too tart.
Use a whisk or fork, at this stage, (either do the trick),
then *slowly* pour and whisk the oil till it is nice and thick.

If you want it *really* thick, machines here can be used –
they blitz so much the molecules all get completely fused.
The dressing that is made is thick and will hold tight for days,
great if you are using it in lots of different ways.

If your dressing doesn't need to cater quite so far,
just put it all together in a simple, clean jam jar.
Put the lid on, screw it tight and shake it really well –
it won't hold long, but that's just fine as, really, who's to tell?
It only needs to hold as long as it takes to be eaten,
which won't be long as what you've made, quite frankly,
    won't be beaten.

how to

make a

Caeser salad

Caesar salad's been around for very many years,
invented to be served to those who'd drunk too many beers.
For it was 1924 when restaurateur Cardini
saw his drinkers needed something salty, crisp and creamy.

Caesar was Cardini's first name, hence the dish became
known as Caesar's salad once it gathered all its fame.
Cardini's base was Mexico and this was Prohibition,
which meant that those who *did* find drink were hellbent on
   their mission.

Cardini's staff were overrun and this salad was able
to be prepared and quickly served right at the diner's table.
The leaves were left whole to be picked up: this was finger food
(an image now that folks with forks might see as rather rude).

In with the leaves were croutons baked or fried in garlic oil,
tossed in dressing made rich by an egg just quickly boiled.
Some final drops of Worcester sauce, some grated
   Parmesan cheese
were all the things that Caesar needed for his dish to please.

It should well be – with so few things – there's no room
   for confusion,
but since that point there've been a lot of Caesar-salad
   intrusions.
Our hairy little salty friend, the punchy anchovy,
was not, for instance, in the dish when made originally.

When it was crucial to get made and served with speed
   and haste,
the drops of Worcester sauce were thought to bring enough
   big taste.
This sauce now tends to be left out, it has been superseded,
as once the anchovies are there it's pretty much not needed.

These fish are now so integral, they're salty and intense,
that no one even thinks they need a case for their defence.
They should, however, be mashed up, their place is *in*
   the dressing;
laying them upon the leaves, out flat – that is just messing.

They're there for flavour, not for style, their role is not
   to garnish –
a rule that's just as true for other things that try to tarnish
the winning Caesar salad list, so simply finger lickin'.
It should *not,* for instance, have on it a great big hunk of chicken.
Grilled halloumi, salmon steak, these things are all a NO!
Prawns and eggs and bacon cubes, these things all have to go!

However tasty these things are, they do *not* have a role,
they were not there in Caesar's 1920s salad bowl.
Leaves get torn or roughly chopped (but this we understand –
for eating with a knife and fork is better, now, than hand).

Romaine should be the green of choice, no need for small,
    soft leaves,
and no to shavings – grating only – when it comes to cheese.
While shavings fall off from the leaves, it's gratings that will cling
onto the dressing, on the leaves, it's this that will then bring
the *substance* to the Caesar salad: it's what makes this lunch,
along with garlic-oil croutons, which bring their
    welcome crunch.
(Some think croutons are a no and say to leave them out
but garlic-crunchy croutons, really, are what the salad's about!)

Potatoes are no substitute, here, for the crusty bread.
If you want these, best then just to make Nicoise instead.
Though this, of course, just opens up a whole new fresh debate:
what is okay - and what is not - upon the Nicoise plate…

how to make

hummus

Hummus is a dip that many people eat each day,
a favourite desktop staple (with a pot of crudités).
It's creamy-nutty-moreish and it's good for general health,
so what is often stopping someone making it themself?

In theory it's so easy, it's tahini and chickpeas
blitzed and mixed with lemon juice: a nice, big, hearty squeeze.
But though the theory's simple, it's a spread misunderstood,
and what gets served as 'hummus' is, too often, *not* so good.

Debates abound about what sort of chickpeas can be used;
the role of olive oil is, often, *really* quite confused.
So, let us sort some basics out, our hummus Ts & Cs,
the things we need to do to make the most of our chickpeas.

First things first, the chickpeas, then: are dried and
    canned okay?
It turns out, yes! That both are fine and work in their own way.
Dried beans are seen as 'real deal', they need a night-time soak
(but this degree of planning might not well suit quite all folk).

Once they've soaked, they can be drained and transferred
    to a pot
with a little pinch of baking soda: really, not a lot.
A little goes a long way to help soften up the skins.
This is, for creamy-dreamy hummus, such a secret win.

Cover them with water then you bring it to a simmer,
skim the scum that forms upon what's soon to be your dinner.
Leave alone, to cook like that, aim for half an hour
until they're nice and soft to touch (but not yet turned to flour).

(If canned is what you have and want then this will be just fine:
just drain and simmer in fresh water for a little time.
Fifteen minutes is enough to soften up their bite –
don't skip this stage, it's quicker – much – than
   soaking overnight).

Either way, a pinch of salt can now be added in
(don't add it at the outset, it will toughen up the skins).
Drain the beans but save the water, though it's not good-looking,
it tastes divine when added to the next soup you are cooking.

Put the beans, while they are warm, into a mixing machine.
Blitz them well, to form a paste (it's yet to get its 'sheen').
Next, it's time to add your creamy, rich tahini paste –
unless you've got the bitter kind, which frankly is a waste.

This is the crux: the cause behind a hummus-making quitter.
It is too thick and stiff – tahini should not taste that bitter.
It needs to be all smooth – the texture should not be like sand.
It needs to be a creamy, nutty, Middle Eastern brand.

The next thing that is added in, is some fresh lemon juice –
the paste will freshen up with this and start to feel all loose.
Garlic, salt, and then what's truly worth its weight in gold
is adding in some water with ice cubes so it is *cold*.

The meeting of the frozen cubes and warm chickpeas is great,
the melting of the cubes then makes the chickpea mix aerate.
Keep the mixture blitzing round for longer than you think;
it wants to start to look like something you could almost drink.

For once the water's added in a slow and steady stream,
it starts to look as smooth and thick as freshly just-whipped
    cream.
For *this* is hummus, light and fluffy, creamy and all warm –
the shop-bought stuff won't know, from here, how it was
    ever born.

Only once it's on a plate and spread out nice and thin,
is the time the role of olive oil is welcome in.
For olive oil is something to be drizzled on the top –
recipes that say to add it in the mix should STOP!

For this is what will make your hummus claggy and all dense –
on this point there is no room for sitting on the fence.
And that is that! Serve up with bread to help with all
    the mopping.
Hummus should be made at home, not brought home
    with your shopping.

how to make

an omelette

Let's start with chef Escoffier, a fine place to begin:
'Zee omelette is where eggs are scrambled, and held in a skin.'
('Coagulated' was his word but that sounds gross to eat,
and omelettes are the most delicious, simple, supper treat.)

There are so many different ways an omelette comes to be,
but, when it comes to types, they can be grouped into just three.
The first type is quite thick and flat, the whisked-up eggs
    soon find
their role is equal to the things they help to set and bind.

Tortillas are a classic here – they're loved all over Spain;
frittatas are the same (except they have a different name).
Asian omelettes – also great – and last (by no means least)
the veggie-herb-packed *kuku sabzi* from the Middle East.

The second omelette sees the egg whites whisked in such a way
that once they're folded with the yolks, they cook up like soufflé.
The texture is, as a result, all fluffy and so light
the air inside means, also, that it gets some lovely height.

The omelette that excites the most opinion by far
is number three: the fancy French one – rolled like a cigar.
This is the one we will address as people like to preach
the rules they have and principles they want to share
    and teach.

Eggs, first off, should be the freshest you can find and source.
Butter is important here so that's fresh too (of course).
If you like a thin omelette then, per person, it's two;
three works well – it has more heft, the choice is up to you.

Depending on the quantity of eggs you are to choose,
a vital factor is the pan you are then set to use.
If too large, the eggs will spread out crêpe-like and too thin.
If too small, the sides get tough, whilst it's not set within.

A twenty-centimetre pan, for two eggs, does the trick.
And most will vote, if there's a choice, for pans that are
    non-stick.
Some will say to be the true and *very real* deal
you should be only using pans which are made of French
    steel.
That is fine so long as it is seasoned *really* well,
don't do this and you are left with stuck-on eggy hell.

Eggs should be room temperature, cold take too long to set,
(which means a base all overcooked is what you will then get).
'Whisk the eggs till just combined', say those who take
    some care
to make sure that their eggs don't fill with fluffy, foamy air.

Some will add some liquid here, the choice will just depend
on if you like to eat a fluffy omelette in the end.
For if you add some milk or water this, when cooked, will mean
the water, when it hits the pan, turns straight into hot steam.
The steams acts like a leavener as steam, of course, will rise:
a fluffy, risen omelette will appear before your eyes.

Some think such additions are a no-no, frankly moot!
As adding milk or water only means the eggs dilute.
This crew prefers a firmer feel and think it good to savour
the concentrated, richly yellow, purely eggy flavour.

Either way, it's butter next, which must melt in the pan.
A tablespoon per omelette, so start with the best you can.
The pan needs to be hot enough as what you want to get
is for the eggs to quickly cook and for a skin to set.

The butter's foam should be reduced (but not starting to brown).
If too hot, that's fine, just quickly turn the heat right down.
There are two ways the omelette maker's process can now go:
it can be cooked real hot and fast or lower, so then slow.

If you want to make it fast, you must release the brake.
The eggs go in and, straight away, you tilt that pan and shake.
The bottom will then start to set and scramble in the middle.
Sides come in – up, down, left, right – it can be quite a fiddle.

For just as it begins to set, you tilt the pan away –
the omelette's folded into three (if that worked, well done – yay!)
If you want to dial it down (this need not be a race),
you can still make an omelette at a slightly slower pace.

In this case you leave the eggs alone so that they can
begin to set before they are then shaken from the pan.
An edge is lifted up so liquid egg runs underneath.
Repeat till set, then fold and plate and eat (with some relief).

There are still those who like to make a song and dance about
the fact that spatulas should be an implement left out.
The thinking – that the texture's ruined – was shared by
   Julia Child
(though what she used to flip and jerk did look a *little* wild).
So down your tools if wrists are strong (as in, they're made
   of steel),
the rest of us can fold away and keep things nice and real.

For most of us are neither French nor fancy or that chic –
our eggs are what we crack and cook to get us through
   the week.
We are not TV chefs, quite yet, we make these when our mood
requires some simple, comfort, easy, frugal, French(-ish) food.

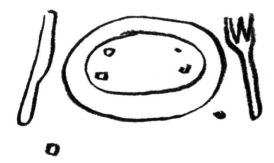

a note on how to cook an omelette –
Elizabeth David, 1932

In terms of 'secrets', there are none. To make this omelette fine,
we can quote from the famous *Omelette and a Glass of Wine*.
Elizabeth David shares a note from proprietress Poulard
who wrote that making omelettes is, by no means, tough or hard.

'I break some good eggs in a bowl and beat them really well.
I put good butter in a pan, add eggs and shake like hell.
I add some cheese, a little cream, and then I tip the pan
first one way and then the next: the egg moves where it can.

Do this 'til the eggs are set but in the middle runny.
Fold in three, with palette knife: from there to plate and tummy.
Keep the filling minimal, some herbs chopped nice and thin,
omelettes are no substitute or stand-in for the bin.'

The quote above is not *exactly* what was in her letter.
The gist is true and, really, omelettes don't get any better.
Though the note was written out in nineteen thirty-two,
it has the roots of all the things we are still told to do.

how to

peel

and

crush

garlic

part one: how to peel

Before we even start to crush and think about our meal,
we need to free our garlic cloves and then they need a peel.

Getting them off from their head needs one sharp knife
    and twist –
in it goes, between two cloves, and then turn with the wrist.
This works well if what you need is individual cloves,
as bashing down the whole head flat would free the lot
    in droves.

Once you've got your cloves out, you are set, soon, to begin.
before you get to crushing, though, you must remove the skin.
This is done in lots of ways – let's limit it to four:
'knife blade', 'rolling', 'shaking', 'steaming' (though there can
    be more).

For the 'knife blade' it is crucial that the blade is wide,
for it is turned and used to crush, once it is on its side.
This removes a lot of skin but not quite *all* of it,
you'll need to use your hands, as well, to get the final bit.

Next is 'rolling' in two hands (or tubes, as well, work fine).
The downside here is only one clove gets peeled at a time.
It also means, if rolled by hand, the smell – it really lingers!
The garlic will be there whenever nose comes close to fingers.

A third way, then, to peel the cloves is with a great big 'shake'
between two bowls – one up, one down – metal, so they don't
   break.
Once inside you shake like mad, you *really* make a din,
after which you'll see that most cloves have popped from
   their skins.

If that all seems like too much work, then effort can be saved
by popping cloves into a bowl to then be microwaved.
This means the cloves will 'steam' inside and loosen from
   their skin,
the paper rises up as steam comes through and settles in.
The garlic cloves are being cooked behind the oven door,
so don't do this if what you want is garlic staying raw.

So when it comes to peeling garlic, don't get too confused,
different ways work best, depending on how it gets used.
Whichever way you chose to peel (and different ways will suit),
it *always* helps to first slice off the little firm end root.

part two: how to crush

Once it's peeled, you're set to crush, so long as you're convinced
that crushing is what will work best (not chopped or sliced
    or minced).
For how you mash your garlic up depends upon the plan,
for how it's cut affects what happens once it's in the pan.

If it's crushed and to be cooked it will brown really fast,
its taste will spread throughout the dish, from first bite to
    the last.
So if you want to dial things down then it is best to slice –
the flavour's then a background note, all mellow, mild and nice.

The difference here in strength of garlic is to be explained
by all the crushed and broken garlic little cell membranes.
These membranes are made up of compounds in which
    sulphur waits,
ready to be let right out once crushing activates…

So when it comes to crushing garlic, there is strength of feeling,
even more than chats about how best to do the peeling…

Starting with the garlic press, this is a 'love' or 'hate'.
Those who love, and make the case, proclaim 'It is just great!
It's quick and easy and you also end up with some juice,
and it's no bother getting that last bit (which is stuck) loose.'

Those who 'hate' feel really strongly that the garlic press
wastes the garlic once it's crushed and stuck there in a mess.
They say a kitchen gadget should have many different roles –
that it is not enough to just pass garlic through its holes.

They cite the kitchen knife and say this does the job just fine,
as well as being useful in the kitchen *all* the time.
With a knife you finely chop then scrape to form a paste –
a method that just needs some salt and ends up with no waste.

Those who doubt this 'knife-scrape' method are the ones
    who think
that doing this will mean the chopping board will really stink.
A board is bigger than a press to wash away the reek,
and scraping with a knife also requires some knife technique.

A method that requires no board or knife or garlic press
is pestle, mortar, salt and bashing, to which some say, 'Yes!
There is no waste as all the garlic stays within the bowl –
the juice, the flesh, it's neither stuck nor left in any hole.'

Others think it's just more kit, the washing up's a pain,
thinking that it's better to just use a microplane.
It is still 'kit' but kit which does not take up too much space
(and it's great, as well, for grating hard nutmeg and also mace).

Doubters of the microplane say, 'Good luck to your knuckles!
Once they're grated off as well, there won't be many chuckles.
We'll trade a bit of washing up, to save ourselves the threat,
for shaving off your knuckles is a thing you don't forget.'

The garlic-crush debate is one that truly never tires,
so choose the method that you like and that the dish requires.
Just keep a check on size of clove, they can be *really* vast,
so whatever way you crush or peel, the smell will *always* last.

how to make pesto

Pesto alla Genovese: the green sauce that is found
in Genoa, in Italy (the word means 'crush' or 'pound').
A jar is found in nearly every kitchen, every home,
yet it's such a simple sauce for us to make up on our own.

You need to start with basil leaves: one hundred grams is nice,
and basil's super sensitive, so pick the leaves – don't slice!
For when you slice up basil leaves, they quickly oxidate,
which means they will go dark and brown and really not
    look great.

Some will think it's only right to make the sauce by hand,
but others get that time is short and fully understand
that leaves, once picked, will be blitzed up inside a food machine.
But don't blitz yet! We want to keep things nice and vivid green.

We next add in some pine nuts: forty grams or so will do.
Before you add them, have a nibble of just one or two.
For nuts can turn quite rancid – if they have a bitter taste,
just cannot be undone, so throw them out – they are a waste.

It is a pain to chuck them out; it's true, they are not cheap.
But other nuts are fine if pockets are not feeling deep.
Cashew nuts or walnuts can be used (though here, of course,
be careful: don't still claim this is a 'true' Genoa sauce!).

So, taste the nuts: if good to go, then they are added in.
Next you take two garlic cloves (remove them from their skin).
Crush them well, with press or fork, whatever it best takes,
or in a mortar with a pestle and some sea salt flakes.

So, basil, pine nuts, garlic, sea salt: tick and tick, tick, tick.
Extra-virgin olive oil is next in, here the trick
is starting with the best you can in terms of quality,
for how it tastes will impact lots on how the sauce will be.

Ten tablespoons is needed, now you pulse it once or twice.
Keep it coarse – some texture here is really rather nice.
Once it's blitzed the next thing in is grated Parmesan:
fifty grams is needed – finely grated, if you can.

Mix this in by hand from now, you do not want to blitz –
a rubber spatula works well to give a gentle mix.
Then spoon the pesto to a jar and top with olive oil
to stop the oxidation (which would make the colour spoil).

Keep it in the fridge, once made, where it will last for days
to make your pasta pesto (or to use in other ways).
It's great to have with chicken or with vegetables or cheese,
but you have made it – now it's yours – so use it as you please!

how to

make a

tomato

sauce

Tomato sauce is such a useful thing to make and freeze –
batch-cooking is the way to go, it's made with so much ease.
Tomatoes cook until they're soft and left to fall apart,
so why is it, then, seen by some as *such* a cooking art?
It's *because* it is so simple, and the choices are *so few*
that there is room for every cook to say what they would do…

Canned or fresh tomatoes? Well, it's all about the season.
Fresh are only best when ripe, thanks to the simple reason
that ripe means that they have real flavour (that is, they
    are *sweet*) –
the only way they should be, if you care for what you eat.

Better than a tasteless batch is starting off with canned,
but even then there's such a range, depending on the brand.
Those who think their sauce is best say cans are of most use
when filled with peeled, large plum tomatoes packed in their
    own juice.

The benefit of being whole (not chopped into a mush)
is that the cook can then control how far they take the crush.
Starting off with crushed or chopped will be more imprecise,
for this can range from chunky mash to purée or small dice.

(Tomato paste and also purée are a separate thing.
They've been cooked down, they are intense – umami's
    what they bring.
They have been strained, they are processed, they are a
    concentrate,
so any sauce made up of them is pretty *far* from great.)

So with our canned tomatoes, what's the next thing we
    should choose?
Oil or butter? Garlic, onion? Which one's best to use?

Those who always reach for butter as their chosen fat,
like that it emulsifies and for the sauce means that
it stays all nice and creamy – the dairy's sweet and smooth,
as anyone who's made Hazan's tomato sauce can prove.

(Hazan, for those new to her name, is *the* Italian cook;
her famous sauce is published in her 'classics' recipe book.)
All she does is add tomatoes to her cooking pot
with an onion, sliced in half, plus butter (it's a lot).
Cook and crush, from time to time, just at a gentle simmer.
Now you have it! Hazan's sauce, it's *such* a dinner winner.

Butter is not *better*, though, olive oil, of course,
works as well, so get the best that you can buy and source.
The River Cafe, London, talks about how it's the shopping
that's the thing to nail before you even think of chopping.
Extra-virgin olive oil is more than worth its price.
the link is real between the cost and how the oil tastes nice.

The River Cafe's recipe – a leader in its field –
starts with oil and onions, finely sliced (and peeled).
They cook them for a long time, i.e, *really* low and slow,
to make them soft and sweet and with a golden-yellow glow.
Stirring them from time to time, and moving them around,
so that they get all nice and soft, while never getting browned.

What starts as harsh – an onion – a thing that brings a tear,
gets to the point where it will melt and almost disappear.
When the cans are opened, and once they're added in,
the sauce then cooks for quite some time, so that it won't
   be thin.

Once the onions are soft, garlic's added too:
thinly slice or finely chop or crush – it's up to you.
The difference is that thin slices will bring a flavour burst,
while crushing means the garlic flavour will be more dispersed.

After that it's just a case of seasoning the pot –
salt and pepper, sugar too, it doesn't need a lot.
Just a pinch to balance out the fruit's acidity:
taste it first and then you'll know how much 'a pinch' should be.

Once you've made your basic sauce, you need to taste
    and tweak,
it will be different every day and from each week to week.
Have a batch all ready and line up the Tupperware:
one for pasta, one for pizza, one to have as spare.
It is so reassuring, when you know that stocks are high –
that supper can be made without the need to think (or sigh).

how to make

mayonnaise

Home-made mayo is a sauce that often gets berated
for being 'troublesome' to make, for being 'complicated'.
But, really, can it be that hard, there's only so much toil
involved in whisking egg yolks with some water and some oil.

'Oh yes', say those who've tried (and failed) with home-made
    mayo-making,
'the sauce just splits, it curdles – yuck! – it always ends
    up breaking'.
'Thinking it won't work, won't help: envisage sauce success',
say those who know these things work best without
    predicting stress.

An understanding of the sauce can be a place to start,
for knowing how it binds will help it *not* to fall apart.
The sauce is an emulsion, it is oil and water gelled,
two things that, when they're left alone, are naturally repelled.

To make them coalesce as one, to make these two things blend,
emulsifying egg yolk is the mediating friend.
Emulsifiers have two ends: their head loves oil (the fat);
their tail, meanwhile, loves water which, for mayonnaise,
    means that
the egg yolk, when it's broken down, will bridge the
    two together
and once that's done – once they're combined – they stay
    that way forever.

Knowing this about the yolk ('fat heads' and 'water tails')
will go some way to making sure your mayo never fails.
It also means you understand the all-important risk
of what can happen if you stop the movement of the whisk.
For if this stops, the bonds won't form, which is a major hurdle;
the oil and water separate, which means the sauce will curdle.

As well as whisking constantly, success will also need
the oil and egg to be mixed at a slow and steady speed.
Remember we are mixing things that are not friends,
    they're fickle.
Slowly does it, hence the need to start off with a trickle...

Another way to help the eggs work as a bonding bridge
is making sure you take them out from being in the fridge.
If they're cold, they're sluggish and they won't emulsify
however much you whisk and whisk – however much you try.

So that's the science of the sauce, let's talk about the food,
looking at the things we need to make sure we include.

Eggs, of course – but should this only ever be just yolks?
There seems to be another camp of 'whole egg' thinking folks.
The increased water doing this (which using white will mean)
tends to be used by those who make their mayo by machine.

In with our yolks we need to add a little pinch of salt
(and put the bowl on a damp towel: so that it will not bolt).
Some say salt goes in at the end – 'its role is just to season' –
but it emulsifies as well, so that is a good reason
to stir it first in with the yolks, this helps to make them thicker,
which helps a stable sauce to form and makes it do so quicker.

The volume of the oil to come, the huge amount you'll use
will show how vital is the oil that you decide to use.
Don't think that it is always best to start with a big hitter –
only using extra-virgin olive makes it bitter.

What you want is something lighter with a neutral taste –
groundnut and rapeseed both work well to make a silky paste.
Once the sauce has come together of its own volition,
then the extra-virgin olive is a great addition.
View it as a flavouring, a finishing rich oil
(knowing that the sauce is stable, so won't split or spoil).

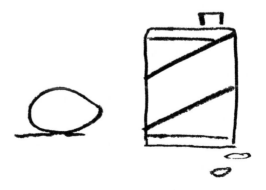

Pour in oil until the sauce is firm (but also loose),
then finish off with vinegar or else some lemon juice.
They both work well so it is fine to here sit on the fence –
use what you have, to spare, around if there's no preference.
Add the acid at the end (if anyone asks why,
if added first it slows the rate the yolks emulsify).

So that is it, the mayo's made, each cook can now decide
what else they want for flavouring, what they now want inside.
Mustard is a classic, either wholegrain or Dijon.
Herbs or capers, anchovies, it's hard here to go wrong.
Try adding lots of garlic (which will then make mayo be
the punchy sauce that is, of course, garlic-rich aioli).

Before we make our mayonnaise, one last thing to contest:
'by hand' or 'by machine', which method works, for us, the best?
Machines can work, they are not 'wrong' (and there is
    little harm
in saving all that whisking work from just one little arm).

The two are not the same, when it is whisked up with a blade,
the texture's more akin to what you get from ready-made.
Those not keen say what results is 'gloopy' (they want 'glossy'),
while team machine retort 'you are just purists being bossy'.

Another way, much loved by some, is with a hand-held stick;
it's proven that it really does the mayo-making trick.
Put everything into a jar (in which the stick will fit)
then let the (lighter) oil rise, and on the yolk it sits.

The stick head must be at the base when it is then turned on.
This is vital, if you don't, the sauce will turn out wrong.
For once the blender is turned on, the egg yolks are first mixed
and then the oil is pulled down in and gradually blitzed.

Mayo is a sauce so simple which we've elevated
to being something to be feared: as 'hard' and 'complicated'.
Try it out (and if all fails, then who are we to kid?
We know you've got a jar back there, the one with the blue lid)...

how to make

hollandaise

Once you get the principles of making mayonnaise,
other egg-yolk sauces are the same in lots of ways.
Though hollandaise is just an egg-based sauce that is
   served hot,
like mayonnaise it's something that is feared quite a lot.

But feel no fear, it's just a sauce. ('It's just a sauce?' some mutter:
it's quite the richest combo of egg yolks and melted butter.
Eggs Benedict, asparagus, these things make so much sense
when paired with hollandaise – there is no sitting on the fence).

When it comes to butter, though, you need to choose a side:
you either start with whole butter or else choose clarified.
Whole butter has some water in it, which is what then makes
the sauce get thinner as it's whisked (which can mean that
   it breaks.)

Butter that's been clarified (that's drained to form pure fat)
thickens, on the other hand, which for the sauce means that
it's not at all diluted: it is firm and strong and stable
(an outcome that some would not choose, though, even
   were they able):

'For hollandaise should be a sauce that can pour from a jug,
not something that should sit inert and upright in a mug.
If you like it thick, then clarified's the one to use,
but butter makes it silky-smooth so that's the one we choose!'

Either way, the sauce should spread out onto a cool plate
before the egg yolks overheat and then coagulate.
Heating yolks so that they're thick but don't turn into curds
is more a case of practising than learning just through words.
But words are what we have here, so they are, for now, our tools,
to list the ways that hollandaise is made. What are the rules?

A really common method is to use a bain marie.
If anyone is nervous then this method ought to be
the one that is first tried out, it is rather slow but neat,
keeping eggs from curdling through distance from the heat.

A heatproof bowl sits perched upon a simmered-water pot,
the bowl base should not touch the water (which will now
    be hot.)
The egg yolks go inside the bowl, some water then, be brisk!
As melted butter gets poured in, you also need to whisk.
The distance from the water means that it can take some time
to thicken but it's not a race so everything's just fine.

Second is the 'Carême method'. This one's for the pro
who wants to get a hussle on – there's no time to be slow.
The eggs and water sit directly in the pot to meet
the flame below, which is, of course, an intense form of heat.
Once they start to thicken, next the butter is whisked in –
the butterfat's emulsified, the cooked eggs start to thin.

The plus point for this method is it's really very brisk,
but carries with it what for many is the real risk
that starting with a small amount of egg (which then
    gets cooked)
means that it will be scrambled by the next time you
    have looked...

Lastly, there's a method that is simple and works fine.
Just put it all into a cold pan, all at the same time.
Heat it gently, stir to cook and soon the sauce will be
what you want in terms of thickness and consistency.
It almost sounds too simple, as though there must be a trick,
but there is not, it's safe and sound (and also pretty quick).

Whichever way you make it, you must take it off the heat
as close to serving as can be when you are set to eat.
For, as it cools, it loses all its silky-butter powers
so hollandaise is not a sauce that likes to sit for hours.

(and then)...

Once you've made your hollandaise, this sauce is known as
    'mother',
from which you can then easily and quickly make another.

Béarnaise, for instance, is a classic one to make.
It's rich and aromatic (and pairs really well with steak).
Starting from the 'mother sauce', what makes this so sublime
is adding in some vinegar and concentrated wine.

The combination cuts through all that butter: it seems wrong
how much can be consumed with some nice, fresh, green
    tarragon.
A grind of pepper, chopped shallots and you will quickly feel
as though you're in a bistro with a gastronomic meal.

Sauce Maltaise is, likewise, one step on away from mother.
Orange juice is added, so it's sweeter than its brother.
Sweet, but also tangy, this will very often be
served with veg – it works so well with heads of broccoli.

There are a lot of other little, smaller, punchy sauces
taught on all those classic, French-style old-school
    cooking courses.
Some are made with meat glaze or a red tomato paste,
whipped cream, cayenne or Dijon, experiment and taste.

For once you have your 'mother' you are free to have a roam,
knowing that, if you get lost, you're never far from home.

how

to

cook

rice

One rice and another rice do not cook up the same,
the rice that we are looking at is 'standard' white long-grain.

Unlike brown rice, which includes the fibrous bran and germ,
white rice, which is purely starch, is just the endosperm.
This speeds along the cooking time (which will not be that long)
but, still, this is a dish that many find they can get wrong.

Before we cook, it can be useful to outline our aims:
our goal is fluffy, separated, light and distinct grains.
We do not want them mushy, yet we do not want a 'bite',
we want them somewhere in between – we want them, well,
    just 'right'.

Our rice will be cooked on the stove and cooked inside a pot,
for which we have a lid and water that we will make hot.
Other ways are there that will still do a proper job,
but we are sticking to the one pot and the standard hob.

First things first, we rinse the rice, to lose its starchy coating.
(You only need to rinse long-grain – it is maybe worth noting –
for with short-grain you *want* the starch, think creamy,
    rich risotto,
which happens from the starch released that has not
    been let go.)

Soaking is the next thing for your rice to end up great,
for cooking rice is largely getting rice to rehydrate.
And soaking softens up the grains, which helps the water in,
this speeds up things, which when you're hungry, is a
    dinner win.

Once it's rinsed and soaked (and drained) the next thing
    we must know
is what our water to rice amount is – what's the ratio?
One-to-one parts water to rice, by volume works out great,
with quarter part of water more, which will evaporate.

You might need more, you might need less: you will soon get
    the feel,
depending on the strength and tightness of pot lid and seal.
The tighter that the seal will be, the *less* extra you need
for what is there will not evaporate with such great speed.

Bring the water to the boil, then turn down very low.
Seal the pot and let the rice cook really nice and slow.
Don't remove the lid at all, just let the rice grains swell –
twelve minutes, steaming, for basmati always works so well.

Fluff the grains up with a fork then reseal and let rest
for at least five minutes for your rice to be its best.
Fluff – don't stir, for if you stir the rice up in a rush,
the swollen starch grains break apart and will become a mush.

This combination of boil–steam is just one way to cook,
there are so many other ways, enough to fill a book.
Par-boiling first in lots of water, followed by a steam,
is what a lot of people go for: they're the 'two-pot team'.

Others find the extra pot to be a wash-up pain.
They might cook rice as if it's pasta: simply boil and drain.
Pure steaming works best for the likes of sticky
    short-grain rice,
for long-grain it is not well suited, so won't end up nice.

All of these alternatives have fans, they are all fine.
The boil–steam way, though, hits the mark and works out
    every time.

So that's your perfect rice, which is now ready to be paired
with all the stews and curries that you have (have you?)
    prepared...

a chicken

A 'simple roasted chicken', well, it's simple till you look
at all the many choices you must make for your roast chook.

The oven heat, for instance: does this start up, then go down?
Once it's started cooking, do you turn the bird around?
Does it start off upside down, or even on its side?
To truss or not: what is the point of legs all neat and tied?
Is brining really worth it? Spatchcocking feels *intense*!
Rinsing first to then pat dry: does that make any sense?

You think you'll have a read around, to see what others say,
but every cook and chook does things a *slightly* different way.
They whisper on their tricks and tips to make their
    chicken great,
but all these whispered tricks and tips just serve to complicate…

So let's here try to pare it back: for all you've read and heard,
remember that this *is* a simple, low-key roasted bird.

First things first, it's best to start with free-range top-notch meat.
Spend more, each time, and buy less often: see chicken as
    a treat.
Size-wise, it's one-point-five kilos that feeds a group of four
(so get a little larger if you want to feed some more).

Remove the chicken from the fridge – for just an hour or two –
before it goes into the oven, so it's not cold through.
Let it sit there, as it is, the skin dries in the air.
Use the time to do some things that need to be prepared.

Decisions must be made between a choice of different fats
(some will say to cook with none, but where's the fun in that?).
   Some will favour olive oil, massaged into the skin,
whilst others go for butter mixed with things that also bring
lots of punchy flavour: woody, savoury –
lemon, thyme (they pair so well) – or chopped-up anchovy.

Either way, the butter needs to get right to the flesh.
Lift and loosen up the skin (as if it were a mesh).
Fill the space with butter, it will make the meat so moist
(a word that makes things great to eat, if not one so well voiced).

Don't forget to also take the time to really season
(this would be the only thing, if skipped, that would be treason).
Salt and pepper – on and in! – for seasoning will be
what takes the flavour from the skin right to the cavity.

About the oven temperature, now people get *obsessed*.
But ovens vary in each home and you know yours the best.
So don't get lost upon this point or you'll miss the wood
    for trees –
just know that you are going for one-ninety-*ish* degrees.

If you start too high, the meat will quickly just dry out,
but if you go one-ninety, you can stick right here throughout.
The challenge is we want our birds to have two different things:
tender, juicy chunks of meat and crispy golden skins.
If you want to start it higher and then bring it down,
do this if it works to help your skin crisp up and brown.

Obsessing here, most will agree, is something of a waste,
but no one will dispute the need to very often baste.
Spooning over juices, which are sitting in the pan,
is – in terms of crispy skin – the thing that really can
ensure it browns up nicely to a golden-salty-brown
(it also stops the need, oh joy, for cooking upside down).

How long to cook the chicken will depend upon its size –
check it's done by sticking a sharp knife into its thighs.
The juices running must be clear: if seeing any pink,
return the chicken to the oven, have yourself a drink.

A 'regular'-sized chicken, just to give a little guide,
once it's in the oven, needs one hour and ten inside.
Remove it from the oven and then let it have a rest,
it's this that helps your chicken be its tender, juicy best.

Fifteen minutes, sitting out, will be completely fine –
time to make the gravy (or to crack on with that wine).
Take a moment, raise a glass and mark things with a toast
to all the things that are so great about a Sunday roast.

how to

roast

a potato

Whatever else is being cooked up for the Sunday roast,
potatoes are the thing, when nailed, that cause the cook to boast.
A tray of crispy, roasted spuds – all fluffy-soft inside –
is, indeed, a happy sight and source of well-earned pride.

So what's the secret formula? What are we all to do?
To bring about a crispy skin and make sure they're
   soft through?

First of all you need to know the texture of your spud –
you want the starchy, floury kind (and scrubbed of all its mud).
Maris Piper, Desiree, these are both well-known names.
King Edwards, Cara, Duke of York, they all cook much the same.

The thing they share is lots of dry starch in their separate cells,
which, when cooked, will separate and it's here (when it swells)
that what we want, in terms of texture – fluffy, fine and dry –
will be produced, thanks to the starch, whose levels are so high.

Portion-wise, allow a kilo if you're feeding four.
This allows for seconds if some want a little more.

Peel and cut them knowing that the thing about this veg
is that you want to maximize the corners and the edge.
For these are what will crispen up when meeting fat and heat –
a combination that will make these tatties hard to beat.

Before we get to heat and fat (and dripping versus oil),
we need to help our spuds along, they need a quick par-boil.
The purpose of the par-boil is that, if they're cooked from raw,
the outer skin – just paper-thin – will soon be crisp no more.
For it will quickly soften as the moisture seeps right through,
so building up a starchy layer will be the thing to do.

Really salt the water well and start with it from cold.
(Though starting with a simmer is what sometimes we are told.
Heston does this, for example, but he also takes
his spuds so far they fall apart and everything just breaks.)

Timing-wise, some say four minutes (which can feel rushed).
Heston goes for twenty (which just makes for that big mush).
Eight to ten is where most think you can't go too far wrong.
Drain (and save the water for the gravy later on).

Next we leave our spuds alone for just a little while –
spread them on a tray or rack (for if they're in a pile
they will not dry or firm up, which are both a real must
if we want to maximize the crispness of our crust).

Next we need to rough things up, the step to clearly prove
that oil and fat need lots of cracks (not for things to be smooth).
For cracks are where the fat goes *through*, you need this
    little break –
put them back into the pot, then give the pot a shake.
Not so much that they collapse, more that they just get bruised
(this is better than a fork, which some say is best used).

Nigella here adds semolina to her par-boiled wedges,
loving that this brings a sweetness to her crunchy edges.
On this point, there are a lot who aren't on the same page,
they find the semolina grainy, so they skip this stage.

Whilst all this is going on, it's most important that
your oven's on and heating up a large tray with some fat.
For once they're cooled and roughed a little, it's the time of day
that spuds are ready to be spread out on the roasting tray.

The oven should be really hot, though estimates can vary,
from one-eighty to so hot that it is, quite frankly, scary.
Either way, spread out your spuds, they do not like a crowd,
for this means that they'll steam (not roast) and chef will not
   be proud.

Toss them quickly, so they're coated, close the oven door.
Leave them be, they do not really need you anymore.
Turn them once, just halfway through: no more! Be in no doubt,
your spuds will not improve if tossed and turned again
   throughout.

The best fat used for roasting will elicit firm-held views.
The truth is that there are a lot of options you can use.
The benefit of using fat saved from a goose or joint
(in addition to its flavour) is its smoking point.
Being high means it's okay and will not burn or spoil,
as is the case if using extra-virgin olive oil.

Extra-virgin, by itself, is heavy and a waste.
Butter too, if used alone, will make for a burnt taste.
If you want to use these two, they work when they're combined,
so long as what you start with is the lighter oil kind.
Veggie oil is also fine – use groundnut or rapeseed –
for a leaner, crispy spud, these are all you'll ever need.

How much oil or fat you need to put into the tray
differs from each cook to cook, so there's not just one way.
Some say 'just a little'; i.e., 'barely more than dry',
whilst others go for so much that their tatties oven-fry.
Such opposing viewpoints are no reason to despair –
just use enough to coat the spuds, plus one more slosh to spare.

How long they take to cook, of course, depends upon the heat:
they always take a long time, so work back from when you'll eat.
For golden roasties are a thing to eat at their peak-best,
which means they do not want to sit around for long or rest.

For though we talk of 'humble spuds', they're sensitive to time –
the bird or joint and other veg will have to fall in line.
The veg can be reheated and the meat can rest and wait,
it's the tatties that must quickly get onto the dinner plate.

how to

make

gravy

Once your chicken's roasted and it's sitting on a plate,
it's gravy-making time (the chicken likes to rest and wait).

There is no need for recipes or how-to manuals
(nor is there need to reach for any stock-cube granules).
For when it comes to gravy needs, it's very hard to beat
the residues and juices that have come straight from your meat.

Though gravies can be dark and thick, or amber-gold and thin,
they all start out from what is right there sitting in your tin.
For gravy is a way to stretch the sediment and juice,
thickened with a little flour (unless you want it loose).

For what you want means that two gravies will not ever be
quite the same in terms of flavour or consistency.
So, while a 'master' recipe is pretty hard to find –
there are some basic principles quite good to bear in mind.

First of all, you need to get the juice and most fat out –
leave a little fat in there; a tablespoon (about).
Save the juice (and save the fat), these are not for the bin.
Prepare the pan and, after that, the juice will go back in.

To get the pan 'all set', the first important thing to do
is scrape the solids off the base, get all that sticky goo.
The flat end of a spatula will lift it all, then once raised,
some water, wine or stock goes in – the pan is now 'deglazed'.

Pour this liquid in a bowl; again this is to savour.
It's liquid-gold, all packed with huge amounts of fatty flavour.
Spoon a little fat back in – ten grams should do the trick –
with equal weights of flour (if you want to make it thick).

The pros and cons of adding flour splits up the gravy crew;
there is, sometimes, a prejudice, towards those making roux.
The sense is that this 'thickening' is somehow 'not quite right',
that it will make it gloopy (when it should be nice and light).

'Gloopy gravy only happens if there is too much',
say the flour sprinklers, as they add *just* a touch.
'It also only happens at the next stage when you whisk
the liquid back into the pan and if you are not brisk.'
Gravy that is flour-free will lack the oomph to coat.
Jus this ain't – we serve it up in something called a 'boat'.

Either way, back to our pan, the liquid has returned,
bringing with it all the flavour of the brown-bits-burned.
Sit the pan straight on the hob and heat it from below,
stirring as it simmers, somewhere medium-to-low.

Once the flour (if it's used) is whisked in and dissolved,
the liquid can now be increased, the flavours be evolved.
The way to up the liquid is to add more liquid in:
stock or water (with some wine) just poured into the tin.

The liquid here, added in, can really change the taste.
Water is okay if you are cooking in a haste,
but if you want your gravy to be more than simply 'fine',
a well-made stock will more than pay for your invested time.

Making stock would take us down a whole new rabbit hole,
suffice to say that, gravy-wise, it's got the starring role.
The flavour in the stock is key as this will then translate
to all the gravy that will soon be poured onto your plate.

Whether you have added stock or water with some wine,
the crucial thing is that you keep on tasting all the time.
Tasting and assessing and then really paying heed
to what your stock is lacking, and to where there is a need.

Add a little lemon juice if tartness is required.
Or if it's sweetness lacking, then some honey is desired.
Jelly, sugar, apple juice, or even good balsamic
all work well added to the gravy if it's tasting tanic.

If you think you need something with flavour spare to lend,
soya sauce or Marmite are your trusted flavour-friends.
Umami is their middle name, so they will do the trick
of turning up the flavour dial and giving things a kick.

So with our gravy in the pan, our stock and cooking juices
simmer on so that the liquid thickens and reduces.
Taste it one more time and if not there, what is the reason?
Fix the flavour, it might only need a final season.

Put it in that gravy boat or just a little jug,
put it in a tea pot or a nice big drinking mug.
Boat or jug or pot or mug, however you may pour.
the only question you should hear is 'Please, can I have more?'

how to cook a steak

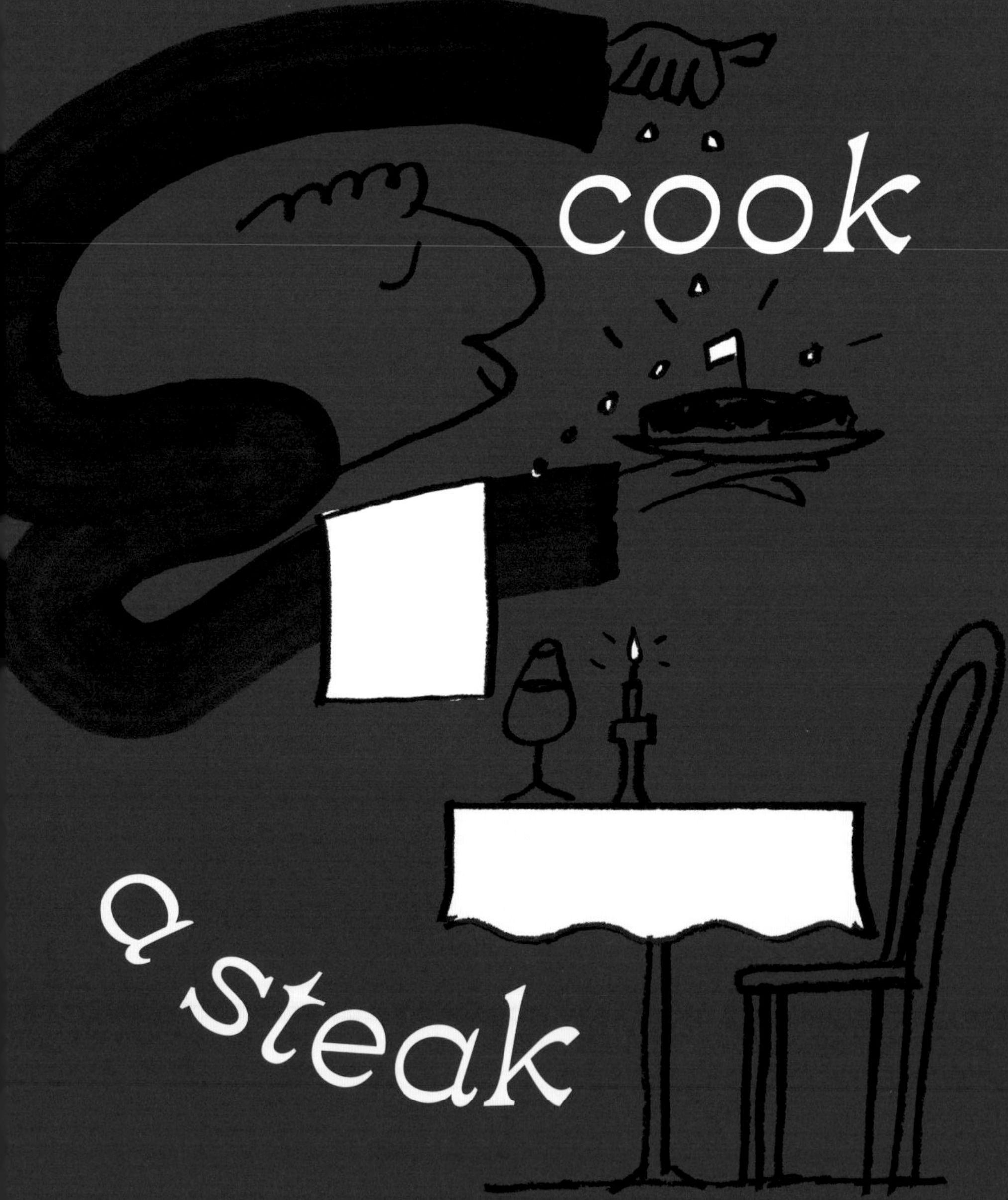

It's something that takes minutes, to be grilled up in a pan,
yet steak is something that we often leave to 'those who can'.
We think it needs a pro-chef, one to show us how it's done,
but steak can, really, be cooked well by (nearly) anyone.

The first thing that you need to sort is dry-aged,
    first-class meat –
it's not a thing for 'everyday', it is a special treat.
When it comes to cooking steak, no two cuts are the same,
so first of all we need to know a bit about each name.

part one: know what steak you're cooking

If you want a cheaper cut (that is not second rank)
bavette is what you want to get (it's also known as flank).
It is a thrifty cut that looks just like a flattened sheet
(or some say rope) but when it's cooked, it's delicate to eat.
It must be cut against the grain and works well thinly sliced.
It makes a stunning salad (and is, as we've said, well priced).

Onglet is another steak that likes to be cut thin –
it's not a melt-in-mouth cut, though, so for some not a win.
If you want a melt-in-mouth cut, if you want it tender,
you also need to be a pretty uncomplaining spender.
For tender meat comes from the parts of cow least exercised –
the less time worked, the more they are the parts we tend
    to prize.

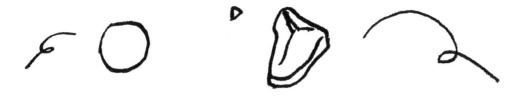

Tenderloin or fillet, these are both a first-rate cut,
coming from the middle part, a long way from the butt.
For at the butt (and also front) is where the cow works most,
so things like shoulder, arm and leg are best cooked as
  slow roast.

Sticking with our tender cuts, which many seek and savour,
they'll be, for others, something of a compromise on flavour.
For tender cuts are often lean – and lean, of course, means that
they lack the swirls of marbling and nice thick layer of fat.

And fat translates to flavour, as we see when in the pan,
the 'marble' melts and buys the chef some time in that they can
then leave the steak there, on the heat, to get a solid crust
(something that, for many, is an absolute steak 'must').

Rump's a classic choice for this, with steaks cut pretty thick –
they need six minutes in the pan, so nothing madly quick.
Rump is, for some, too 'chewy', though, you need to use
    your teeth,
and, yes, it is a cut that tastes like you are eating *beef*.

Sirloin steaks come from the back, around the lower middle –
they're nicely marbled, with some fat, so cook best on the
    griddle.
The griddle pan here needs to be as hot as it's in hell,
so this could be one left to restaurants to do really well.
It is the steak for 'city boys': 'I eat, therefore I am
a big and clever (slightly old-school roaring alpha) man.'

Next up's the massive T-bone, it is part of the sirloin.
The T-shaped bone means that the separate cuts of meat
    will join –
a fillet on the one side and then, when it's off the bone,
a sirloin steak – it's two for one, do not eat this alone!
The two meats cook at different rates, hence tough to get
    just right
(another one best left to chefs who cook steak every night).

It's better, really, choosing rib-eye, cut thick, with bone in,
which means that it will not dry out (as it would do cut thin).
For rib-eye, with its tasty fat, needs heat but also time,
so cooking it requires a careful treading of this line.

part two: know how to cook the steak you are cooking

To keep the inside really juicy, and to char the crust,
there are some rules which everyone agrees are a must.

Steak must not go straight from fridge into a red-hot pan,
so leave it out a while; for an hour, if you can.
A water bath can also work if you are pressed for time;
leave it in its shrink wrap or else clingfilm should be fine.
Either way, don't skip this stage, whatever else you do –
a steak, if cold, will burn before the middle is warmed through.

Next we need to season well, that's *really* liberally,
though everyone has different thoughts on when this stage
   should be.
Some say it should be done first to let the salt sink in,
while others say it's best to do it just as you begin.
For once the salt is on the meat it draws out beads of sweat;
osmosis means the steak will then become a little wet.
If it's wet it will not char, this thinking makes good sense,
as beads of sweat get in the way – they act as a defence.
Because there is no cavity, that also is the reason
to do it long before so *all* the meat can get a season.

Next you need a heavy pan: cast-iron (though it's dear)
is the one that helps your steak to get the strongest sear.
For being heavy ups the energy the base contains,
which makes the steak feel like it's being cooked by
   actual flames.

The pan is hot, the meat is on, so now you need to wait
(there is to be a lot of smoke, so you should ventilate).
The next stage will depend upon the steak that you
   are cooking,
so all of them rely a lot on touch and, also, looking.

part three: how to tell your steak is done – 'the rule of thumb'

All steaks vary just as much as how you like it done,
but you can tell a lot by what is called 'the rule of thumb'.

Take your thumb and index finger, press them both together –
the muscle at the thumb joint feels a bit like loose, old leather.
This is what your meat will feel like if you want it rare.
If you want to take it further, leave the pan right there.

Press your thumb and middle finger: now the palm feels firm.
This is one along from rare: just practise and you'll learn.
The next along – the ring finger – when pressed against
    the thumb
is medium (the little one means that it's overdone).

Some think this all just complicates the whole thing far
    too much,
that nothing beats just practice and, as we have said, the touch.
Despite such protestations, though, it pays to get the knack,
as it is such a quick and useful, easy, 'handy' hack.

part four: and finally…

The question of steak flipping, is the thing that is up next.
It gets the steak-crew flippin' mad (and those at
    home perplexed).
Some swear that steaks should only ever be turned
    halfway through;
others say it's fine to flip as much as you want to.

Both camps claim their way is best; the flip-lots thoughts
    are voiced
by those who say that frequent turns are what will keep
    things moist.
For turning really often means that both sides of the meat
are stopped from either taking in (or letting out) much heat.
This means the meat cooks faster and then won't
    be overdone –
an outcome to avoid, agreed upon by everyone.

It all depends – it always does! – upon the cut of meat.
A bone-in rib-eye needs, for instance, to stay put on heat.
Just sit it in a hot pan and then leave it, do not fuss.
Wait six minutes, flip it once, to form a golden crust.

Six more minutes after that, then take it from the heat,
add some butter to the pan and baste it on repeat.
Add some herbs – thyme sprigs work well – and garlic that
    is crushed,
then move it to a chopping board, things must now not be
    rushed.

If there's one thing upon which every steak chef is agreed,
it's that it's vital now to rest, the opposite of speed.
For this is when the juices settle, thicken and sit tight,
staying there in place until that first, delicious bite.

Use the time to finish off now all the other things:
the creamy spinach, thick-cut chips or crispy onion rings.
For as with all the steak debate, you'll still be told it's wrong
to skip Béarnaise and choose, instead, some mustard
    from Dijon.

Some want some crispy salad leaves, served up with
    fresh baguette.
Others like a pan sauce (those who like to serve things 'wet').
Everyone has perfect pairings, but it is your steak night,
so cook and eat the steak you want, there is no wrong or right.

how to make pastry

Let's start with a disclaimer, for this is *not* to be
a comprehensive 'how-to' guide on French pâtisserie.
We are not making strudel dough, cannoli gets the chop,
go buy your Danish pastries from a lovely, local shop.

For laminated pastries, with their layers, folds and turns
are not a thing the home cook, truly, *really* needs to learn.
Shortcrust is the useful one, the place where most will start,
for those who want to make a pie or quiche or simple tart.

Though pastries all have lots in common (they're the same
    in that
they are a mix of flour, liquid and some sort of fat).
The range of pastries then stems from the way these things
    are treated:
how much of what gets used and if it's cold or if it's heated.

Hot water pastry, for example, as the name suggests,
likes things warm, whilst others need the fridge for
    frequent rests.
For a puff or flaky pastry, fridges are a must
as they are for anyone who's making some shortcrust.

So, when it comes to shortcrust, the fat is cold (thus hard).
Some use butter (best for flavour), others will choose lard.
Lard, though best for texture, is for flavour quite a waste
because (compared to butter) it has very little taste.

Butter, though, has water: it's about a tenth in weight.
Lard has none which helps the dough, when cooked,
    to separate.
This separation makes the dough then crumble perfectly
and crumbly is the way we want our shortcrust dough to be.
A mix of lard and butter is a thing that lots will do.
To get the best of both worlds you will need to use the two.

Water is the liquid added, drizzled nice and slow.
Add as little as you can to form the basic dough.
Even though it might seem as if there is not enough,
any more will mean, when baked, it shrinks and ends up tough.

Tough is quite the opposite of how shortcrust should be:
we want it to be *melt-in-mouth*, to be all crumbly.
This will happen when the pastry maker gets to know
how vital it is *not* to overwork the pastry dough.

The more a dough gets overworked, the more gluten appears,
and gluten forming is what shortcrust pastry always fears.
For when we come to take a bite it should crumble apart,
so particles all small and 'short' are wanted from the start.

Another way to help the pastry gain its crumble power
is taking time to really rub the fat into the flour.
With the tips of fingers or a processing machine,
the fat coats all the grains, which then, in turn, will also mean
the gluten growth's restricted, a thing which is a must
for making pastry that will crumble *and* still be robust.

The flour used is one that is quite low in its protein –
plain (all-purpose), has you covered, it's the shortcrust dream.
Double up the butter weight and that is what you need,
the ratio is one-to-two (so memorable indeed).
A little salt, if wanted, just a pinch is fine and right,
but bear in mind that too much salt will make the pastry tight.

So that's our basic shortcrust, though there will always be folks
who like a richer pastry so will choose to add egg yolks.
Eggs yolks are like the water, though, in that the dough will find
it likes as little liquid as is needed *just* to bind.

Another variation is to make the pastry sweet
for those who like their pies and tarts to be more of a treat.
The flour, fat and liquid here all have their usual role
though icing sugar's added with the flour to the bowl.

Lard is not a player though, butter rules supreme,
egg yolk, milk or water or a little bit of cream.
A teaspoon of vanilla or some grated lemon zest,
play around to make your sweet shortcrust how you like best.

Before you set out making lots of shortcrust in your home,
know that pastry has a mind all of its very own.
So even when you think you've done things absolutely *right*
the pastry can come out all *wrong*: chewy or too tight.

Don't despair, just have a little run through of the list
to make sure there is not a resting stage that has been missed.
For resting plays a crucial role, it helps the dough relax,
the gluten strands chill out, the butter hardens to its max.

Another reason for the dough to be tough or to shrink
is if it's been so overworked it's gone beyond the brink.
For if you really go for it with all your heart and hands
you are just making lots of stretchy, twisty gluten strands.
These will then bounce back when they go in the oven heat
and 'bouncing back' means 'shrink' which means 'it does not
    look too neat'.

Another explanation, if the crust is hard to touch,
is that the water added has been too fast or too much.
For though it makes the pastry feel and roll out really great,
all that water will, when cooked, soon just evaporate.
The drier dough – more hard-to-handle – at the pie's outset,
means tender, shortcrust pastry is, once cooked, what you
    will get.

If the bottom of your crust is rather soggy and quite pale,
this means the blind bake stage has been a quiet, total, fail!
A soggy bottom can't be saved but, once done, it then means
you won't forget to bake it blind, next time, with blind-bake beans.

So practise here makes perfect, you must make it once or twice
and don't forget the filling must also be *very* nice.
Whether it's an apple tart or classic quiche Lorraine
shop-bought pastry never will quite taste the same again.

how to

make

strawberry

jam

'Making jam is easy!', those who often make jam say.
So why do they all make it in a *slightly* different way?
It's the *slightness* of the differences that discombobulate,
so let us get some jam facts sorted, let's get some ideas straight.

Jam is simply crushed-up fruit that's cooked and turned to gel.
Four simple things are needed to ensure that it's done well.
Sugar is the first thing, but in order to then set,
strawberries need some extra things, which you will need to get.

The fruit is low on pectin (that's the plant world's natural glue),
so pectin must be added, ways of which there are a few.
Strawberries (low on pectin) can be mixed with fruit like quince
(tart apples, grapes or blackcurrants would do the same
  job since
their pectin levels are quite high, which means that you
  are getting
all the power of their 'glue', which helps the jam's firm setting).

Another way of introducing pectin to the pan
is using sugar called 'preserving' or there's 'sugar jam'.
The differences between these two does not always seem clear,
but jam sugar (which has more pectin) is what you will use here.

So fruit and sugar and pectin, the fourth thing that we need
is the presence of an acid which slows down the speed
with which the sugars in the jam will start to crystallise
(an outcome which rules out the jam from winning any prize).
The acid can be tartaric (the powdered real deal)
or just add a bit of lemon juice, along with lemon peel.

So even with just these four things it's not feeling that 'easy',
it's not just 'fruit and sugar with a little lemon squeezy'.
For every ratio must be right for these things to match,
you'll need to play around with each and every different batch.
For everything depends upon the fruit with which you start.
This is science! This is maths! Much more than it's an art!

So let us say our berries weigh a neat, round one kilo,
how much sugar do we need? What is the ratio?
Some say that it is one-to-one – that's easy, right and neat –
but others say this makes for jam which is just *far* too sweet.
They'll lower down the sugar to around six hundred grams.
"*A less cloying and looser jam*" will claim its many fans.

So, let's get on with cooking once our fruit is in the pot.
Do we cook it low and slow or do we boil it hot?
First things first we bring the crushed fruit to a gentle boil,
then we pour our sugar in, but for it not to spoil
we stir it gently, with heat low, until it disappears
(if it boils before that's done, lumps forming are the fears).

To help the sugar disappear, a useful thing to do
is to spread it on a large tray and then gently heat it through.
This means that when it meets the fruit it's warm and good to go
and once it's all stirred in, things can then speed right up
    from slow.
For once it's gone, the heat's turned up and at this stage,
    the trick
is to really boil the jam up, hot and fast and very quick.

Saucepan-wise, there are some things which make it more ideal:
a mouth that's wide, which has low sides and made of
    stainless steel.
These all help the fruit cook fast, which is imperative
for it to set and to make sure that nasties do not live.
For bringing fruit up to the boil will make it sterilise,
which means that it will not grow mould (which would be
    most unwise).
The jar the jam goes in must also be completely clean:
just put it through a hot wash in the dishwashing machine.

The length of time the fruit gets boiled may well, in fact, just be
the thing where there is *such* a range and such discrepancy!
'*Just five minutes*,' says one person, then the next will say
that '*forty-five is needed*' for the jam, if made their way.
As with lots of data sets it's safe to take the mean,
so go for something in the middle, round about fifteen.

Setting a fixed time, though, is not really how to get
the jam you want – that's only gained by 'testing for a set'.
If you have the means to check, it's 'one-o-five' degrees,
but most of us will use a saucer placed in the deep freeze.
Chill a little blob of jam, then push it with your finger –
when you pull it back you want the jam to stay, to linger.
Wrinkles on the surface are another indicator,
if not there, then cook it more and check two minutes later.

Now you're set the jam goes in jars (which are clean
   and warmed),
once you've skimmed the surface scum (if there is any formed).
Adding in a tiny bit of butter here appears
to make sure that the scum which is there
   somehow disappears.

Seal the jars well – use a clean lid – so that there's no doubt
that pesky mouldy-making microbes are kept firmly out.
Stick a pretty label on and join the jammy crew
who claim that making jam is *such* an easy thing to do!

how to

make a

martini

People take this seriously, their steps and preparation,
for what is meant to be a simple, classy, clean libation.
When it comes to choices, there are five things to debate:
the questions that determine and decide martini's fate.

The first one is the biggest (or the place where things begin)
'do you want it made with vodka or, instead, with gin?'
Some prefer the vodka for its smooth and neutral taste,
while others think that 'neutral' is another word for waste.

They want a drink with flavour, and it's the crisp and
    complex notes
of gin – which tastes of juniper – which, for them, wins all votes.
Presuming that it's gin which we are going, here, to choose,
the next decision is *which* gin should be the one to use.

London Dry (that's Beefeater) is fine for a safe bet,
but those who are discerning might prefer, instead, to get
something bold like Tanqueray (it's dry and loved by pros),
or Hendrick's, with its background notes of sweet and
    perfumed rose.

The second question, for our cocktail, with which we are met
is 'what extent you want it to be 'dry' compared to 'wet'.
For, with your gin (or vodka) you will need some
    white vermouth,
what 'some' will mean, proportion-wise, here speaks the
    drinker's truth.

Ratios can vary lots, they go from one-to-one
to those where vermouth quantity is, for the most part, none.
For those who go for 'none' the drink is only fit to pass
when vermouth is just used to pretty much rinse out the glass.

A little drop is added, maybe, just one drop is fine
of this fresh and fortified herbaceous dry, white wine.
(Churchill, it's reported, always thought it would suffice
to simply look at Vermouth as the pure gin hit the ice.)

Now the ice is broken, we can move on to point three.
For how cold it should be served, is a factor which is key.
For if not Arctic-cold, the gin can burn upon the throat,
and all that gets experienced, is gin's harsh, fiery note.

The fact that gin and glass should be based in the cold
    deep-freeze
is a point upon which everyone just plain agrees.
The fridge is fine if you don't have a freezer with the space.
There are still ways to keep a straight martini-serving face.

This moves us on to question four – it's one we have all heard –
and that's if it's to be a drink that's shaken or just stirred.
Though Bond would have it shaken and the line is one
    we quote,
the method makes no sense, in truth, so wins no
    thumbs-up vote.

As it's only spirits here, there is no need to shake.
For there's no juice to mix in and there's no egg white to break.
In order to get full control of chill and ice dilution,
martinis should get stirred, it is the common sense solution.

Sorry, Bond, to call you out, but that's how it should be,
whether you are Daniel Craig or old-school Connery.
The drink is now set to be strained into its cocktail glass,
leaving just one question for the drinker to be asked.

'Would you like a lemon twist or olive in to garnish?'
(For some the very concept is, quite frankly, just a tarnish.
For this is seen as 'dirty', with its strong and salty brine
and 'dirty' is, depending on your viewpoint, 'dream' or 'crime'.)

But whether yours is dirty or you like to have it dry,
after one you'll feel as though you are all set to fly.
Though one more round might seem to be the best of all ideas.
It's not! Stop there! We all know that this night will end
    in tears...

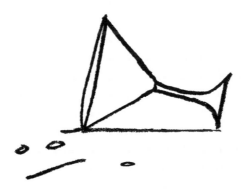

how to host

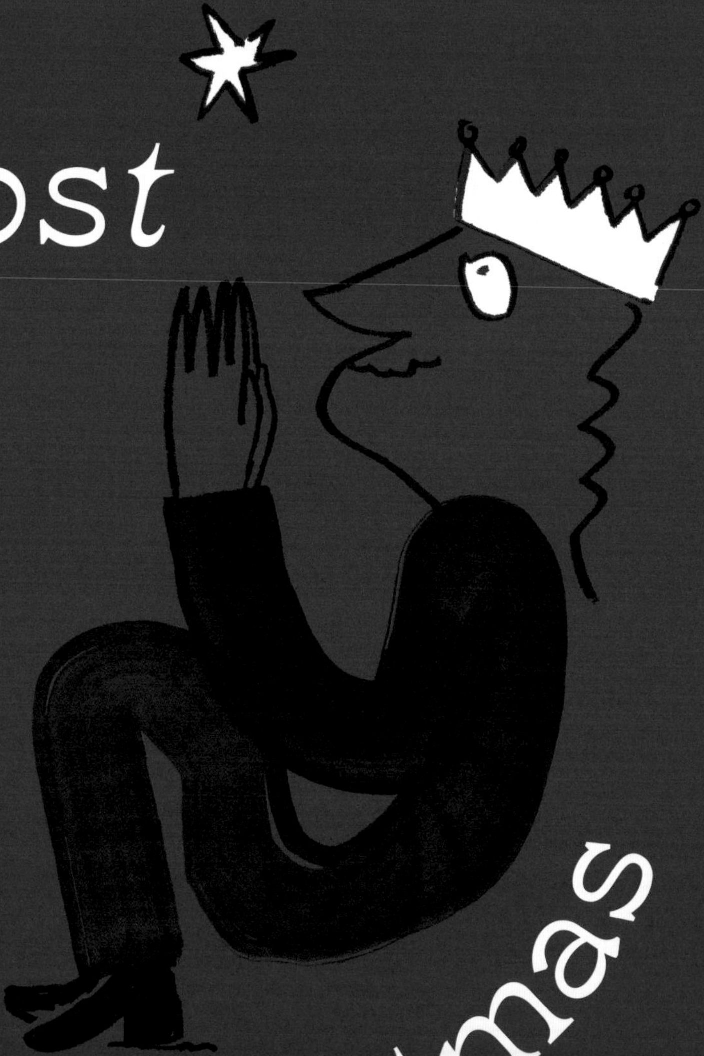

Christmas

(a short guide to staying sane)

If you're hosting Christmas and you're having family round,
here are twelve tips to help your festive feet stay on the ground:

1. The first top tip (and it's the most important one by far)
   is that you should remain the cook and person that you are.
   Even though there is a lot of build-up to the day,
   it doesn't mean that you should do things in a different way.

2. Get stuff in the freezer, also get stuff in the fridge.
   Make some space, just shove it in (we know, it's all a squidge).
   Once it's in, its job crossed out – it's something that is 'done',
   and once it's crossed off from the list there's more time to
     have fun.

3. Once you've planned your menu, all the food that will be made,
   stick to schedule, make a plan, hold tight and don't be swayed.
   For in the Christmas run-up, there are endless 'good ideas',
   but block them out – your menu's great! – do not unleash
     those fears.
   What you planned when planning, when just sitting in
     your kitchen
   will still be great, will still work well, maintain that
     first conviction!

4. Make some time to practise what you plan to eat and cook
   however great and failsafe your skills and Christmas book.
   The only way to guarantee your food will all taste nice
   is if you've practised in advance just once (or maybe twice).

5. It's not the time in which to reinvent the very wheel.
   It's just a simple roast, remember, try to keep it real.
   With a few more sides, of course, than we would tend to make,
   plus a few dried-fruit-filled pies, along with Christmas cake.

6. When it comes to Christmas cake, please cut yourself
    some slack –
    no one minds a mince pie that has come out of a pack.

7. Ditto Christmas pudding, is it really worth the pain?
    The reason people want it, frankly, is just for the flame.

8. Buy a great big Stilton, add some walnuts and some dates.
    Put them in a few nice bowls, that Stilton on a plate.

9. Fill the whole fruit bowl with lots of lovely clementines,
    the smell and sight is one of festive, citrus-happy dreams.

10. If anyone asks, on the day, if there's a job to do,
    say 'YES there is, there really is, there are, in fact, a few!'
    Everyone should have a job, it will be a non-starter
    if the host assumes the role of angel Christmas martyr.

11. Guests have come for lunch, remember, not to see
    you stressed.
    They've come for fun, not for some food that feels like
    restaurant-best.
    Far better for the host (and food) to be served up all chilled
    than aim for 'perfect' at the risk of someone getting killed.

12. So, in short, don't be crazy, it's that 'ho-ho' time of year,
    when all that's really wanted is a little festive cheer.

Recipes, as we have seen, should be viewed as a guide.
Instructions to inspire the cook, not rules to which they're tied.
For recipes can fail to say the things we *should* be taught:
the principles to help with general culinary thought.
So here to end this recipe-less, recipe-ish book,
some rules to be a bold and happy home-based general cook.

The most important rule, by far, is make sure that you season.
If food has little taste, then this will surely be the reason.

Veggies like a *lot* of salt, they also quite like oil.
They love some heat – try roasting things that you might
   tend to boil.

Speaking of that oil, it does not thrive in heat and light.
Keep it in a cupboard, in the cool and out of sight.

Onions will *always* take a long time to sweat down.
Up to twenty minutes if you really want them brown.

When it comes to breakfast, reach for savoury (not sweet).
Choose eggs and herbs and lots of coffee: eat, sleep and repeat.

Buy a granite pestle and a big, sharp kitchen knife.
Small or cheap or blunt ones will not have a long shelf life.

When you are out shopping, if you see some proper scales
(digital) get hold of them – you'll save on baking fails.

When it comes to baking, do not try to improvise,
the use of spoons to measure, if you want things right, is wise.

If you're new to baking, you must do what bakers say.
When you're cooking savoury, there is some more leeway.

Aubergines taste best when they are charred on open flame.
Doing this will really up your 'cooking veggies' game.

Capers are a winning combo with all sorts of fish,
and anchovies should be involved in every chicken dish.

Poach or roast a chicken weekly; make and use the stock.
(Or 'bone broth' as it's called by all the new kids on the block.)

Always make a little more than you think you will need,
then put half in the freezer for a future – welcome – feed.

If, when tasting food, you find that something has gone wrong,
try a little squeeze of lemon, it's a flavour bomb.

Read through all instructions well before you start to cook.
As once you're up and running, you don't want to stop and look.

Take the time to do your prep – all chopped and ready – neat!
You won't have time to slow things down when it's all on
    the heat.

Taste when you are cooking and again before you serve.
Don't hold back on salt – it's all okay! – you've got this, hold
    your nerve.

When it comes to serving up, make sure you do with glee.
No food will be improved by lashings of false modesty.

Be happy that you've cooked and, also, happy that you're able
to gather people that you like to sit around your table.

They've come to sit and decompress, they're in a happy mood.
They've come to see *you* (not to judge your cooking or
    your food).

So sit down, too, it's time to set aside the oven glove.
For food is not about 'the food", it's all about the love.

acknowledgements

A book full of rhymes about recipes, with no actual recipes in it, was not the most obvious pitch. The fact that this one saw the light of day is hugely thanks to the following people.

To Charlie Brotherstone, my agent, and to Gilly Smith, for the initial introduction and for all that you do to champion the stories we all tell through food. To Caspian Dennis, Ariella Feiner, Jordan Bourke, Jenny Zarins and Megan Davies for early-stage chats. To Sophie Allen, for acquiring me, and to Lucy Smith for inheriting me. Lucy: working with you is a total joy. You're such a skilled and supportive editor. Thank you for teaching me, finally, the difference between 'that' and 'which'. To Alice Kennedy-Owen, Ellen Simmons, Stephanie Milner, Komal Patel, Louise de St Aubin and everyone else at Pavilion/ HarperCollins for everything you do to make everyone excited about buying books. To Alec Doherty, your illustrations have exceeded my highest expectations and wildest dreams: massive thanks. You're such a huge talent.

Thanks so much to team Ottolenghi – Yotam, Helen, Cornelia, Sami, Verena, Gitai, Noor and everyone in the OTK – for being such a brilliant and supportive bunch and being so incredibly relaxed about my fingers being in all sorts of book pies at once. Particular thanks to Yotam, for supporting me in so many ways over the years and for repeatedly telling me that I had my 'own' book in me. I'm not sure this was quite what was in mind but there we go.

To Felicity Cloake, Niki Segnit, J. Kenji Lopez-Alt (and all at the Serious Eats website), Alan Davidson, Harold McGee, Samin Nosrat, Nigella Lawson, the Guardian website, Christopher Kimball and Francis Lamb. You've been the first I've turned to and read and listened to in the course of researching my rhymes.

Thank you so much to my friends and family. To Mum and Dad and to my brothers Lex and Justin: did all this nonsense start with those 'raps'!? To Neache and Charlie: for always making me feel like I'm smashing it, even when I'm clearly not. To Iva, Maja and Luka: thank you for letting me show you version 24 of the cover and engaging so much. To Jules, Annie, Sonia and Katherine, for good vibes and candid feedback. This is not Mumsnet – Bea, Mary, Lucy, Sarah and Carenza – so many giggles. Carbonara! To the hive-mind – Lisa, Lucy, Jen, Jess, Debbie, Vicky, Sue, Lou: thank you for not giving up on me even though I'm rubbish at keeping pace with you party-peeps. To Nessa and Katie – long live Friday lunch club! You guys are the dreamy best. To Jessie, Ellie and Win: old friends, like bookends.

To Eleanor Walford: I couldn't have stuck at this without you. Thank you so much for reading all of my rhymes with your clever editing eye. I'll be forever grateful, and relieved, that you were there. Here's to the next 40 years of friendship!

And, finally, to my peeps: Chris, Scarlett, Theo and Casper. You've all spent *significantly* longer than you should have done listening to my rhymes, agonising over book covers, smelling my aubergines and generally putting up with me and my lemons. In return, I get all the best bits: the giggles and the quirks, the top chats and the car discos, the wise words and the chaos. Despite me, you're all incredible.